D1623143

NUN, WITCH, PLAYMATE

HERBERT W. RICHARDSON is Professor of Theology at St. Michael's College, Toronto. He was chairman of the Harvard-Kennedy International Conference on abortion and a member of the United Presbyterian Committee on Human Sexuality. His writings include TOWARD AN AMERICAN THEOLOGY; TRUTH, FREEDOM AND EVIL; TRANSCENDENCE; and THE TERRIBLE CHOICE.

HERBERT W. RICHARDSON

NUN, WITCH,

PLAYMATE

The Americanization of Sex

THE EDWIN MELLEN PRESS
New York & Toronto

First edition: hardbound 1971
paperback 1974

Second Edition: 1981

ISBN: 0-088946-950-4

To Paul Lehmann

CONTENTS

PREFACE

This book presents a general theory of sexuality. The theory has been formulated with several questions in view. (1) Historical: how can we understand such institutions as patriarchy, monasticism, courtly love, and romantic marriage as emerging necessarily through the historical process? (2) Sociological: why is it that sexual feelings and responses are class- and culture-specific, and why does education seem to be the most important factor in changing these? (3) Psychological: what is the specific gratification sought by the sexual impulse, and how is this drive related to our strivings for identity and autonomy? (4) Ethical: by what rule are we to judge sexual acts, and how are these related to human fidelity and integrity? (5) Religious: in what ways is sexual union or renunciation conducive to the sanctification of man?

Such a range of questions must be discussed because there is no single intellectual method that can claim a greater validity than others. A general theory of sexuality must *not* be grounded primarily in one or another academic discipline, but must seek to integrate the methods and findings of many. Most importantly, it must be able to illuminate obscure or enigmatic behaviors and be able to generate fruitful hypotheses. That is what this book intends to do.

But every general theory today—no matter how integrative it seeks to be—still belongs to its type. Therefore, by way of introduction, the theory in this book should be classified as an evolutionary rather than as an essentialist or relativist one. Essentialist theories propose that human sexuality has an essence, or invariably fixed form, that manifests itself under all historical and social conditions. For example, Sigmund Freud advanced an essentialist view of sex—and so sought to uncover Oedipal struggle in *all* human societies. Relativist theories, on the other hand, propose that human sexuality has no fixed form, but is totally malleable. For example, Jean-Paul Sartre argues that the individual is free to create the forms of his own sexuality—and this explains his admiration for the autoerotic imaginations of Jean Genet. Another relativist, Margaret Mead, holds that sexual attitudes and behavior can vary as widely as various societies.

The evolutionary theory I am proposing, however, operates with another set of presuppositions. It denies the essentialist affirmation that human sexuality always manifests itself in fixed and invariable forms. It also denies the relativist affirmation that sexual behavior is totally malleable. Rather, an evolutionary theory presumes that the forms of human sexuality change—even changing into what appears to be non-sexual!—but that this change is not arbitrary or structureless. Rather, it is a change that accords with the dialectical process of history itself—in the course of which human sexuality may lose its form and change into what now appears to be absolutely *against itself.* This is precisely what happened in early Christianity, where the vow of absolute virginity and the rigorous renunciation of sex can be demonstrated to represent the emergence of a higher form of sexual consciousness, eventuating finally in the institutionalization of more complex forms of sexual life.

Theories of sexuality can be essentialist, relativist, or evolutionary; there is a second axis in terms of which they can also be compared. Every theory of sexuality is more or less biological-materialistic, depending upon the weight it gives to non-voluntary factors. So, for example, although Sigmund Freud is an essentialist and Margaret Mead is a relativist, they both agree that the biological-material conditions of human existence determine the form of human sexual behavior. Sartre, on the other hand, agrees with Jung (an essentialist) in ascribing primacy to voluntary-spiritual factors as decisive in shaping sexual life. We can, therefore, classify theories of sexuality into six types, by the use of these axes:

	essentialist	relativist	evolutionary
materialistic	1) Freud Kinsey	3) Mead Malinowski	5) Marx/Lenin W. Reich
spiritualistic (voluntaristic)	2) Jung Karl Stern	4) Sartre/Genet J.S.Mill	6) Soloviev/Teilhard Colin Wilson

Among evolutionists, one may stress either the material conditions of human life as determinative of human sexual behavior—as do the Marxists—or one may stress the evolution of consciousness and human spirituality as the decisive factors. The theory developed in this book is closest to type 6 (the evolutionary spiritualistic type). It understands the evolutionary process to be producing not merely more and more complex forms of material existence, but also more and more complex forms of conscious life—i.e., the realm of freedom and spirit. It seems that this more evolved consciousness increasingly determines the variations of human sexuality—and that the entire process is moving toward the full voluntarization of sex, the complete individuation of persons, and the increasing eroticization of society. Among contemporary American thinkers, the theologian John Cobb and the sociologist Robert Bellah have developed theoretical positions with which these views of mine approximately concur.

Having typed my theory, let me, however, enter a caution. Strictly speaking, the problem is much more complex—and I want here especially to stress the mysterious indwelling, or two-in-oneness, of the flesh and the spirit. The whole argument of this book is that there is such a mysterious union of human sexuality and the human spirit *that each can be transformed through the other.* Man is a plural being, fully present to himself in the body, fully present to himself in the spirit. Each is not only the other's other, but also the other's ego. In this fundamental polarity at the heart of the human being, a dynamic is generated that produces the transformation of man. But more to the point, this is why sexual discipline is the foundation of all spirituality and why spiritual exercises are the foundation of all human sexuality. The uniqueness of human life as embodied spirit is best here known and enacted.

HERBERT RICHARDSON

Toronto
Pentecost, 1973

Some Related Readings

BAILEY, DERRICK. *Sexual Relation in Christian Thought* (New York, 1959).

BELLAH, ROBERT. "Religious Evolution," *Beyond Belief* (New York, 1970), 20–50.

BERDYAEV, NICHOLAS. *The Meaning of the Creative Act* (London, 1955), chap. 8.

COBB, JOHN. *The Structure of Christian Existence* (Philadelphia, 1967).

LEGRAND, LUCIEN. *The Biblical Doctrine of Virginity* (New York, 1963).

LUCKA, EMIL. *The Evolution of Love* (London, 1922).

MARCUSE, HERBERT. *Eros und Civilization* (Boston, 1955).

NEUMANN, ERICH. *The Origins and History of Consciousness* (New York, 1954).

SCHUBART, WALTER. *Religion and Eros* (München, 1941).

SOLOVIEV, VLADIMIR. "The Meaning of Love," *A Solovyov Anthology,* ed. S. L. Franck (New York, 1950), 150–179.

TEILHARD DE CHARDIN, PIERRE. "L'Évolution de la Chasteté" (still circulates only in manuscript; for discussion, see Henri deLubac, *The Eternal Feminine* [New York, 1971]).

WILSON, COLIN. *Origins of the Sexual Impulse* (London, 1963).

Part One

THE NUN

CHAPTER I

Mother of Man

How a man views the world always expresses his own view of himself
—even though he may not be aware of this. The evolution of human
consciousness includes, therefore, the evolution of man in all the dimensions of his being. And, in relation to the problem of this book, the
evolution of human consciousness involves the evolution of human sexuality. The evolution of consciousness creates in man ever-new imaginations of what is sexually "natural" and possible.

It is surprising that, in a day when we can see how far man has evolved
biologically and psychologically and socially, we have not really grasped
the fact that man's sexuality has also evolved. The evolution of human
sexuality has meant the same kinds of variation in human sexual behavior, together with the subsequent reunification of these behaviors into
more complex patterns, that are found in the evolution of other aspects
of human life. How, then, did human sexuality evolve?

The process includes several stages. Most simply, we can say that man
first experienced himself and his world as a harmonious "natural" unity,
where there was no separation between his will and his instincts. Then

comes a period where the human will appears as a power to control, even oppose, man's instincts. Historically, this period coincides with the emergence of the great religions, all of which adopted an ascetic attitude toward the world as the counterpart of their faith in a Transcendent Creator. Finally, there comes a period of reintegration, where man's instinctual life is taken up into his newly established voluntary consciousness thereby being transformed and moralized.

The most important of these transformations of instinctual sexuality is the integration of sex and love. The assumption that love, or moral communion, can and should be totally integrated with sexual desire—and vice versa!—is wholly modern. The notion that without love there exists no sexual desire (for the motive for sexual union is love of the beloved) is rather recent. Even to think of sex and love in this way presupposes an evolution of sexuality that took many hundreds of years of human history. Even to think of sexual desire transformed by moral volition presupposes the long evolution of human consciousness.

There are three major elements in this evolution of human sexuality and the modern unification of sex and love. First, there is a tendency in history toward *the moralization of sex*. In the course of history, the motive power behind man's sexual desire becomes less and less a matter of biological instinct and more and more a matter of his volition. That is to say, in the course of history both sexual initiative and sexual intercourse itself become more and more a matter of human choice and voluntary control. For this evolution to occur, man had to discover and develop a power of intellectual and voluntary self-transcendence within himself. Through this power of self-transcendence, man could first develop a nonsexual sphere of life and then integrate sexual feeling and activity within this voluntary sphere.

The second tendency in the evolution of sexuality is the ever-increasing *individuation of men and women*. This development is the counterpart of the moralization of sex. As man's freedom develops in history, he becomes increasingly aware that he is not defined by his body and biological instincts, but has the power to transcend and transform them. As man's freedom develops, he also becomes increasingly aware that every person possesses within himself the power to become a *unique being*. As this awareness of the uniqueness of every person grows, there emerges a new kind of love: romantic love. Romantic love is that love which presupposes the unique individuality of each of the lovers and which presupposes, also, that the love between two lovers is absolutely incomparable and unique.

There is a third tendency in the evolution of sexuality, namely, *the eroticization of society*. In the writings of Norman Brown—who here draws on Freud—there is affirmed to be a primitive stage of history that is identical with the stage of infantile polymorphous sexuality. The infant, before the emergence of his ego, experiences all bodily activities as pleasurable—and experiences all pleasurable activities as sexual. This can occur because the infant's sexual feelings have not yet been concentrated upon his genitals. The infant is not genitally competent, but is "polysexual." Every mode of human communion can be, for him, a mode of sexual union.

In the historical development of sexuality, as well as in the psychological development that takes place in an individual, this primitive-infantile stage of polymorphous sexuality is transcended. Sexual feelings are, first of all, segmented off into the limited genital sphere. But once this has occurred, the way is open for an expansion of sexual feeling out of the genital sphere so as to suffuse, once again, the totality of human life. This expansion of sexual feeling back into the total body and into the totality of human behavior takes place as a third stage in the evolution of sexuality and leads to the full eroticization of society.

These aspects of the evolution of sexuality presuppose, however, the evolution of consciousness, for man's behavior always is based on a distinctive self-awareness of man himself. To study the evolution of sexuality one must therefore study the evolution of consciousness—for the former is but a manifestation of the latter. Sex is not some peripheral human function, but is the fundamental manifestation of the human spirit. The way that man deals with his body shows how man is conscious of himself and what self-aspirations he entertains. This explains why religions—which are fundamentally concerned with the development of the spirit—are concerned with sexuality and find this realm to be the testing ground of faith. The history of sexuality is, as we shall see, the history of the schooling of the human spirit. For this reason, we begin our reflections by considering the most primitive form of human consciousness: mimetic consciousness, the consciousness of tribal man.

If we look back into history, we find that there are no records describing the "tribal" stage of human life. What we know about this stage comes from two sources: from the study of modern tribes by anthropologists and from the study of our earliest historical records, in which we see implicitly the things posttribal man was struggling *against*. In these earliest records, we see men making a transition from preoccupation with biological power to preoccupation with legal power, from concern with fertility to concern with voluntary activity, from living in a kinship tribal society to living in a town or city.

The psychological development required for early men to break free from their kinship tribes has not been properly appreciated. (In fact, there is some question whether—even in modern societies—this breaking free has fully taken place!) It involves the courage to break free from the family as a source of both personal and sexual assurance—the courage to go forth, like Abraham, from his tribal home of Haran to a new world. "Now the Lord said to Abram, 'Go from your country and your kindred and your father's house to the land that I will show you. And I will make of you a great nation . . .'" (Gen. 12:1 f.). This departure of Abraham stands at the beginning of the Bible, at the beginnings of Western history, for history only begins when man frees himself from total immersion in the cycle of nature and undertakes a life of his own through his own will. In leaving behind tribal life, man discovers that he has another kind of life, or power, within him: the power of his ego, the power of his own will. He experiences his will as the capacity to oppose the customs of the tribe and its survival. When man leaves his tribal home, he subordinates his instincts to his ego; he overcomes his "mimetic tendency."

Man's life in the kinship tribe was essentially "mimetic." This means that his life imitated the biological processes in the surrounding environment. Tribal man accommodated himself to nature, to the place in which he found himself. For example, primitive human sacrifice was one aspect of this *mimesis*. In human sacrifice, as in the yearly death and rebirth of vegetation, a part of the species is caused to die so that the species itself may survive. Human sacrifice is man's way of seeking to live "mimetically," by imitating nature.

To the extent that man thinks of himself as tribal, i.e., as a part of nature, there is no other way he can live except mimetically. His survival involves his total adaptation, his total fitting in, his total participation in his surrounding environment. Tribal man experiences even his own sexuality as part of the natural processes of fecundity around him. "Male" and "female" mean to tribal man the powers of generation in plants and animals as well as in himself. Hence tribal man's sexual activity seeks to imitate, and otherwise participate in, animal fecundity. This is why tribal man does not distinguish animal from human sexuality.

What we today assume to be obvious—namely, that the most important distinction in the biological realm is that between man and animals—runs contrary to the basic assumption of tribal man. For him, the basic biological distinction was between male and female. Man's developing awareness that his own sexuality might be different from the sexuality of animals was a major evolutionary advance. One can see this same development take place in children today as they grow up, for a great deal of evolution is recapitulated in human psychological development. A favorite picture book of my children when they were young was called *Animal Daddies and My Daddy*. To conceive of the human parent-child relation in this mimetic way (i.e., like the animal parent-offspring relation) is consistent with infancy, before ego consciousness has emerged.

A more interesting example, however, can be seen in children from about ages 5 to 8, when the "tribal" distinction between male and female becomes more important for the child than any other. In those years my own children identified more with animals of the same sex than with their own siblings of a different sex. My son felt "closer" to our male guinea pigs than he did to his sister. My daughter identified more with the female guinea pigs than she did with her brother. It was simply assumed by the children that the determination of the sex of any pet was a decision also determining to whom the pet belonged. The children not only did not distinguish between animal and human sexuality, but also felt that sexuality (maleness or femaleness) was more determinative of their identity than their common humanity.

The mimetic consciousness of the "tribal" stage makes man regard himself as a subordinate part of his surrounding world. He feels bound to a certain place. He does not, at this stage, think of himself as possessing a life that originates in his own being. Rather, he thinks of the life in himself as infused into him from his total environment. He identifies the breath in his lungs with the wind that blows across his fields. He feels the power of sexual fecundity in his own loins to be but a part of the power of the same sexual fecundity that causes all living things around him to grow. He cannot conceive that the land on which he lives "belongs" to him. Rather, he belongs to the land; it is the land's life that is in him. Hence, to leave that land would be to commit suicide—it is unthinkable. Abraham, however, dared to leave his tribal land. He could have done so only because he already perceived, however dimly, that the source of his life was not in nature, but in Another.

[In Nazi Germany the government undertook a self-conscious program aimed at causing the entire society to "regress" into the pre-Judaeo-Christian tribal state. The emphasis on individuality and ego consciousness that begins, in the West, with Abraham was attacked by the Nazis as decadent. So, for example, the Nazis denied what is uniquely human in man's sexuality and inculcated the mimetic-tribal understanding of it. The Nazi laws against "Aryan"-Jewish marriages were a consistent extension of their tribal view of life.

Just as they tried to inculcate tribal sexual consciousness, so the Nazis also attempted to inculcate the tribal view of man as "a link in the chain of living nature just as any other organism." The following is from a Nazi book instructing teachers how they should explain biology: "We have said that the student must be led to the conception that Germany is his living space to which he is linked by the bond of blood. We have explained in detail that the bionomic approach teaches that the organisms within a living space are dependent on each other as well as dependent upon the whole and that each link must perform an indispensable function in the total accomplishment. When this insight is applied to the human biotic community, when the future German racial-comrade feels himself to be a link in the German biotic community, the class differences and class hatred cannot take acute forms, as was often the case in the past due to a misunderstanding of the actual bond that unites all estates together. Once every German regards Germany as his living space and feels himself to be a link in the German biotic community, he will be fully conscious of the fact that every individual within the metabolism of the biotic community into which he was born must fulfill his own important task. Thus a supra-individualistic attitude is created which constitutes the best possible foundation for training in citizenship. Indeed, it can be said that it has achieved its deepest fulfillment once this attitude is transformed into action.

"Racial eugenics works in the same direction, namely, the education of the student in a national sense. Although it constitutes the finishing touch of biology teaching, its concepts should from the very beginning permeate all biological instruction in all types of schools, and not be left for discussion in anthropology, which concludes the study of biology. It should be repeatedly emphasized that the biological laws operative in animals and plants apply also to man."[1]]

In moving beyond the tribal state of life, the human male radically changed his relation to the human female. In the tribe, the woman held a position of coeminence with the man. In and through her motherhood, his biological life was continued. Man's "immortality" therefore depended upon woman. Through her fertility the ongoing life of the tribe was insured.

The transition from tribal to urban society involved the displacement of the mother from her position of coeminence beside the father. The preeminent symbol of rule in urban societies is the solitary male, who incarnates the new "volitional creativity" in himself. The "Mother" is thus displaced by the "King."

[Note that the new preeminence of the male is not expressed through the metaphor of "Father," since the "Father" is but the coequal of the "Mother" and shares, with her, in the power of biological creativity. The preeminence of the male over the female is expressed through the metaphor of "King." The "King," as embodiment of the new "volitional creativity," displaces both the "Mother" and the "Father" from their position of coeminence. In the Old Testament, God is "Lord" or "King," not "Father."]

In the Bible, we see the transition from biological-tribal to volitional-urban society being effected. The story of the Old Testament is the story of the emergence of the new institution of kingship and the new living arrangement, the city: the social unit that comes to displace the biological tribe. (Ancient cities were, of course, like our small towns.) The distinctive thing about a city is that it is established through a volition, or a law. Voluntary obedience to this law rather than mimetic conformity to nature is the principle of a city's social organization. The lawgiving will of man rather than his sexual fecundity here becomes the primary creative force.

The Old Testament, as the finished product of a city society, gives theological expression to the evolution of man's new "ego consciousness." In Genesis, for example, God is introduced as creative through his power to speak a command or to give a law. The Old Testament God can be creative by the power of his will alone. It is this power of the biblical God to create alone—that is, without a sexual partner—that is the key to biblical *monotheism.* The alternative to this biblical monotheism was not polytheism, but "bi-theism." By "bi-theism" I mean the belief that the divine creative power is sexual rather than volitional. Wherever genuine creativity is felt to be sexual, this feeling is expressed through the affirmation that there are two ultimate gods, or dual principles: the male and the female. Or it is sometimes expressed through the belief that there was originally a single mother goddess who gave birth to a son (through parthenogenesis) and then took that son as a sexual partner with whom she begot the rest of creation. There are a multitude of variations on "bi-theism," but all suppose that the model of creation and order is sexuality.

Belief in the primacy of *sexual* creation is found in every society where the family is coextensive with all other institutions. Such societies are tribal. In tribes, the family is not simply a procreational group, but also the sole economic, political, educational, and religious group. In tribes

—since all institutionalized roles and activities are extensions of family roles—the *kinship system* is identical with the total social system. Tribes are simply complex, or "extended," families.

In kinship societies the woman has a relatively higher position than the one she occupies in urban societies. (Strictly speaking, there are no societies that are absolutely matriarchal, with women ruling over men.) Tribal societies, or societies that do not differentiate the biological and the volitional-legal spheres, necessarily allow a fuller participation for women in all institutionalized activities than do those societies that separate the economic, political, legal, and religious spheres from the family sphere. The separation of these other activities from the family makes it possible for men to monopolize the roles of merchants, rulers, legislators, and priests. Women, confined now to the family space, can be but wives and mothers. The institution of the city (and urban patriarchy) led to the subordination of woman to man.

Ancient cities were interactions of three social institutions: the palace, the temple, and the wall. In the palace, the king laid down the laws that were the foundation of this new, nonbiological social grouping. In the temple, the priesthood celebrated a ritual that mythically transformed the king's ruling into a cosmic act. This "enthronement ritual" displaced the older fertility religion (with its focus on sexual creativity) from its earlier position of cosmic centrality. At the wall, as in the citadel, men released from agricultural tasks and bound together under legal disciplines defended the city against its enemies (ensuring a peaceful market place) and went out yearly in ritual holy war.

Holy war was war undertaken to fulfill the covenantal-legal obligations that men made with the new monarchical God. These covenants were the means by which men from many tribes united in new supratribal groups. The king ruled over these new legal groups, and his power to rule over them was expressed and strengthened by the ritual of holy war.

War is, first and foremost, a vehicle for the creation of supratribal corporate societies. War—even today—is essentially holy war. As, in agricultural tribes, human sacrifice was required as a symbol of man's identification with the natural biological process, so, too, emerging urban societies required the sacrifice of war, through which men identified with that larger social body in whom, through whom, and for whose sake they now had their being.

[Lewis Mumford points out that even in earliest times the economic and human losses resulting from war far outweighed economic and human gains. And he argues that the urban institution of war is actually rooted in the older "sacrificial magic" of tribal societies. "If anything were needed to make the magical origins of war plausible, it is the fact that war, even when disguised by seemingly hardheaded economic demands, uniformly turns into a religious performance; nothing less than a wholesale ritual sacrifice. As the central agent in this sacrifice, the king had from the beginnings an office to perform. To accumulate power, to hold power, to express power by deliberate acts of murderous destruction—this became the constant obsession of kingship."[2]]

In this time of historical transition to urban life, it is hard for us to understand the awe with which men regarded law, the expression of the new institution of kingship. In Plato's *Republic,* law is named as one of the highest spiritual realities, a reality that every mystic contemplates as he approaches final ecstasy. Law is higher than art and mathematics— for although these can exist in tribal societies (Lévi-Strauss has shown that primitive men do abstract thinking), positive law cannot. Law and monarchical lawgiving are the new creations that enable man to break with the immanent biological order.

The same considerations explain the veneration of law, commandment, and legal covenant by the ancient Israelites. In their view, the creation of law is a divine act and law is the very presence, or holiness, of God in the world (e.g., on Mount Sinai). Law was, after all, the social institution that freed them from bondage to nature. It was the instrument of their Exodus from slavery and their establishment in a new land. It was the foundation of their emerging supratribal identity. No wonder, therefore, that the prophets of Israel battled constantly against the "bi-theism" of the fertility cults, which attempted to wrest creative primacy away from law and return it once again to procreation. The fertility cults showed the continuing pull of primal mimetic consciousness upon emerging ego consciousness. They showed the reluctance of men to give up their older tribal identities for new legal-convenantal identities.

[The struggle against the fertility cults in ancient Israel was primarily not a matter of "prophetic protest" against them, but of the institutionalization of the cult in a central temple. The "centralization" of worship was necessary in order to make the enthronement of the king and his ruling the fundamental ritual. The fertility cults existed where the ancient tribes existed, namely, in conjunction with particular holy places or shrines throughout the land. A concomitant of such cults are the "household gods." For example, see Genesis 31:19 ff. Such household gods are found in many societies even today.]

It was in ancient Israel, rather than in Greece, that the primacy of legal over biological creativity was established in its most uncompromising form. Hence it was in Israel that the superiority of the male over the female was most unequivocally affirmed—a fact that has had unique consequences for the position of women in Western societies ever since. But, precisely because of this development, it was in Israel that the anxiety of the male before the sexual power of the female came to its most acute expression.

The emergence of ego consciousness within men does not mean the elimination of mimetic (instinctual) consciousness. It involves a new kind of consciousness emerging over and above the earlier one. To maintain this new level of consciousness involves a constant struggle against regressing into the old. This struggle, in ancient men, was not simply carried out within themselves, but was also acted out "outside themselves" by their projecting their own mimetic consciousness on the female—and struggling against her.

The evidence of the male's psychological struggle against his own mimetic consciousness is seen, in ancient Israel, in the hostility against and fear of the female expressed in the ritual law. In this ritual law, the male keeps himself separated from the female (and the instinctual sexuality she represents) by the institutionalization of a series of taboos that mark her out as one who is "unclean" and to be avoided, especially during her special sexual functions (menstruation and childbirth). Through these taboos, the male not only separates himself from the sexuality of the female, but separates himself from his own instinctive sexuality. He attains, in this way, a more-than-sexual identity. Through observing this ritual law, the Israelite attains a new definition of himself: as one created not in the image of any biological thing, but as a being sharing in the covenanting-legal power that rules the universe.

In addition to these ritualized avoidance procedures, there were in Israel various manifestations of a male hostility directed against women that sought to reduce her to an inferior status. For example, in the Old Testament the female is not regarded as fully human. Only the male is human, i.e., created in the image of God. The female is considered his property. A second example is found in part of the rationality behind the Decalogue proscription of adultery. A man's wife is like his ox or one of his slaves; hence, adultery is wrong partly because it is a form of *stealing* from another man. It injures not the wife, but her owner. That this is the case is corroborated by the fact that the "owner" of a woman may give another man sexual privileges toward her.

The extreme anxiety experienced by men before the sexual power of the female is seen in Old Testament laws prescribing extreme avoidance of her. In fact, it has been pointed out that the Hebrew abhorrence of homosexuality originated in the disgust felt by men that any male should play, in a sexual union, the part of the female. The Hebrews, writes J. Edgar Bruns, "viewed sodomy as an expression of scorn, and in a society where the dignity of the male was a primary consideration, voluntary acts of a homosexual kind could not be tolerated, for both parties would be undermining the very foundations of a patriarchal society: the one because he uses another man as a woman, the other because he allows himself to be used as woman. The dignity of the male is dishonored by both."[3]

The laws of the Old Testament marked out, in many ways, the preeminent status of the all-male group. Men in these all-male groups were bound together by "spiritual blood ties" (e.g., "blood brotherhood") established through their common endurance of an initiatory ordeal and a solemn covenanting together. The ordeal was therefore a *rite du pas-*

sage whereby males were "spiritually reborn" into the male groups that replaced, for them, the biological family. As a sign of his new condition, an initiate would often receive a new name, which signified that his identity was established within the fraternity. Hereafter he was relatively independent of the mothers and the biological family group.

[In modern societies, boys still go through a male group stage when, in their early teens, they transfer their identities from their biological family to a peer group. This transfer even today involves the kind of avoidance and hostility against the mother that was found in the ancient Israelite "amphictyonies" (i.e., covenant groups). Hence, M. E. Harding points out that "boys at puberty are concerned with competitive games and the acquisition of physical strength and skill, corresponding to the hero task. While their interest in group activity corresponds to the formation of men's societies in primitive tribes, the archetypal significance of such interests is concerned with the separation of the youth from the mother and the establishment of impersonal values and the regulations to govern conduct."⁴]

In societies less complex than our own, the male group is not simply a stage men go through prior to eventual membership in an egalitarian heterosexual society; it may be the highest stage of social evolution. (This was the situation in ancient Israel.) In such societies, men live out their entire adult lives within a male group and their behavior never goes beyond its "covenanting" requirements of absolute loyalty to the fraternal group as the bearer of all values and meaning. Hence the sense of unique superiority characteristic of ancient Israel resembles the group pride characteristic of a modern ghetto band; the sense of absolute loyalty binding together the members of the Mafia resembles the loyalty that members of a college fraternity often feel for one another.

What happened in ancient Israel was that the male group displaced the tribe as the primary social institution. It displaced the tribal family into a secondary position, so that the family existed within the male group rather than vice versa. The Israelite act of covenanting extended beyond the limits of the tribal group to create an "amphictyony"—a legal unification of many tribes. In this amphictyony, the legal-volitional act is absolutely primary and creative. The male covenanting act ("bonding") itself becomes the socially creative institution—displacing the primacy of procreation.

Failure to see the male group as the foundation of ancient Israelite society leads to a misinterpretation of biblical religion. For to the degree that they express the covenant of the Israelite male groups, the religion and ethics of the Bible are formulated with the interests of men alone in mind. The Israelite religion, therefore, is a patriarchal religion that systematically discriminates against women in order to protect the emerging ego consciousness of Hebrew man.

The consequence of this social evolution is that the position of Western women has been much lower than the position of women in Oriental societies. The compensating "gain" (if one so chooses to count it) is that Western man has become more highly individuated, or "ego conscious." The development of this "ego consciousness" in Western man involved him in a struggle against his own mimetic (tribal) consciousness and instinctual sexuality. This evolution is what has made man's relation to his own sexuality a peculiarly difficult problem for the West.

CHAPTER II

David and Bathsheba

WE have considered two stages in the evolution of human consciousness: mimetic consciousness and ego consciousness. In the pages that follow, we shall consider three further evolutionary stages. The five kinds of human consciousness, and the general dates of their historical appearance, are as follows:

1. mimetic consciousness
2. ego consciousness (7000–1000 b.c.)
3. rational consciousness (800–400 b.c.)
4. self-consciousness (1300–1700 a.d.)
5. polyconsciousness (just beginning to emerge)

This scheme is somewhat artificial, the divisions having been selected to illuminate certain key facets of the evolution of human sexuality. These five kinds of human consciousness underlie the evolutionary transformations of *sexual* behavior. Changes in consciousness give rise to changes in sexual behavior precisely because every consciousness includes a characteristic self-awareness. So the way in which man is aware of his world determines his way of being aware of himself and those sexual possibilities open to him.

The evolutionary scheme being used here is a selective *typology*. It is not meant to be a straightforward narration of what happened in history. Rather, it is meant to be a framework in terms of which we can see the correlations of many historical facts. Only as we see such correlations of facts will we be able to understand and to narrate what happened in history. So, for example, my discussions of the male groups, kingship, holy wars, ritual laws requiring the avoidance of women, law, and volitional-versus-biological creativity are not meant to replace biblical history. They are intended to help us better perceive the materials in the Bible so that we can actually understand what is going on.

A second point with regard to the evolutionary process we are considering is that the evolution of human consciousness is not a *linear process*. That is, it is not a process in which the movement to stage three means leaving stage two behind. Rather, the evolution of human consciousness is a *complexifying process*. When man moves on to stage three, he adds something new to what he has been and (to some degree) still continues to be. The evolution of consciousness involves, therefore, the multiplication of "levels of awareness." As a new level is added, it may become dominant and organizational for the others. But it never eradicates the earlier stages. This is why, in Nazi Germany, it was possible for an entire nation—which had attained the general level of ego consciousness—to regress into tribal, or mimetic consciousness. The earlier levels are never totally eliminated in the process of evolutionary complexification.

A third point to keep in mind is that the evolution of consciousness that has taken place during the thousands of years of human history must be reenacted, or otherwise reappropriated, in the psychological development of each individual person. The typical American, for example, must relive, in the process of his growing up, the tribal and male group stages. And he must learn the various kinds of consciousness: mimetic, ego, rational, and self-consciousness.

It is a scholarly question of some significance whether an individual person must actually go through all the stages of human evolution or whether, once various competences have evolved, he can acquire them in some new way. I myself believe that once men become self-conscious, they are able to learn the various competences that have evolved in history without actually having to go through, all over again, every individual stage. Once we become self-conscious, we can find new ways to learn things. But this is not a question that concerns us directly in this book. It is enough for us to keep in mind that the process of historical evolution must be reenacted, or *otherwise reappropriated,* in the psychological development of every person. Hence, whenever I am speaking about an evolutionary development in the historical past, the reader may ask himself what might correspond to this development in the psychological maturation of a person today. Or, to reverse the matter, whenever I speak of a psychological development, the reader may ask himself what historical evolution seems to parallel it.

The reason we are relating the evolution of human sexuality to the evolution of human consciousness is because the kind, or "level," of consciousness in a man determines what he can imagine as possible for himself. This fact is an axiom from which my argument in this book is developed: "Every level of human consciousness includes a characteristic self-awareness." We have already considered some illustrations of this axiom. We saw that when tribal man experienced nature as a cosmic process in which he was totally immersed, he had no sense of himself as an individual. He had no consciousness of himself as a distinctive being; he had no ego. He thought of himself as a part of, and therefore resembling, the world around him. His consciousness of himself and his world were fused. He did not know where he ended and his world began. He thought of himself mimetically, i.e., as a being resembling something that was not himself. This psychological condition, which I have called "mimetic consciousness," is described by the anthropologist Levy-Bruhl as *participation mystique.*

Participation mystique may be said to be a mysterious interchange or continuity between separate entities because they are psychologically identified with one another. For the primitive man, like the very young child, has no definite boundaries to his psyche—everything that happens is both in himself and in the object;

he feels with the animals, the trees, and so forth. . . . Before the "I," the *autos*, has been established as a center of individual awareness, the child has no personal consciousness, but exists in a condition of identification with his surroundings. This state of affairs is to be seen particularly clearly in the infant's relation to the mother. He lives in complete *participation* with her, and she is related to him in a similar way though to a lesser degree. Even after he leaves her womb, the infant is still entirely dependent on her and so partakes of both her physical and her psychological condition. After the child's physical dependence has been outgrown, this identity with the mother persists as a psychological reality. For in the unconscious the psyches of mother and child have no clear dividing lines. He is contained psychologically within her all-embracing protection until he has won his freedom and his psychological independence.[5]

We have already considered how man's evolution beyond *participation mystique*, or mimetic consciousness, required a transformation in the way he controlled his sexual behavior. We have seen that overcoming this *participation mystique* involved man's psychological separation from the Mother—a psychological separation that was assisted by the actual physical separation of men from women as they banded together in their male groups. In the male groups, a man developed his will to maintain himself separate from the Mother, and gradually this emerging will, or ego, in man became the dominant mode of consciousness. The triumph of this ego consciousness occurred in ancient Israel, where males now defined themselves not as biological beings, but as beings constituted by the *invisible* power of the will.

The evidence for the fact that the men of ancient Israel no longer thought of themselves in biological, but in volitional, terms is the Old Testament prohibition against portraying God in any image or likeness "of anything that is in heaven above, or that is in the earth beneath, or that is in the water under the earth" (Exod. 20:4). What this prohibition means, of course, is that the ancient Israelites conceived God as different from anything in biological nature. What is often forgotten, however, is that the prohibition against thinking of God as like any biological being included, as its corollary, the prohibition against thinking of the human male as a biological being. For the prohibition against making an image of God also meant a prohibition against making an image of man—since man was understood by the Hebrews to be made in God's image.

The development of ego consciousness in the male groups finally resulted in man's attaining a new conception of himself. He began to think of himself as a being who was more than merely biological. To think of himself in this way involved, of course, a change in his sexual behavior. The key development assisting the emergence of ego consciousness, the key to membership in the male groups, was *the practice of male virginity.*

There is a general taboo within our society today that makes it almost impossible for us to understand why the practice of virginity is necessary in order for a person to achieve ego consciousness and to separate himself psychologically from his mother. This taboo is, essentially, the incest taboo. It is the taboo against recognizing the degree to which the pleasures and practices of sexual intercourse are simply adult reenactments of an infant's body interaction with his mother. Any one of us can become aware of this fact—if he truly wants to. But the point is perhaps more safely made by quoting an authority. Theodore Lidz, chairman of the Department of Psychiatry at Yale University Medical School, points out that "The sexual act contains a definite and direct relationship to infantile relatedness to the mother, with a renewed interest in sucking, in odor, in skin eroticism; and a reawakening of old forbidden desires to explore and play with orifices."[6] In sexual activity, therefore, a person experiences once again the psychological feelings of his infancy, the feelings of his pre-ego-conscious state. "The proper carrying out of the sexual act and the enjoyment of it," says Lidz, "involves an ability to give way to the irrational, the timeless, the purely animal: it includes a loss of individuality in temporary fusion with another."[7]

Lidz speaks, of course, from the point of view of a culture that has institutionalized ego consciousness as the normal state of being. In such a culture, one can speak of sexual intercourse as a "giving way" to the irrational. But how would one speak of this "giving way" in a culture in which the normal state of consciousness was already diffused in a *participation mystique?* In such a culture there can be no "giving way" to the irrational. For in tribal culture, ego consciousness does not yet exist. Ego consciousness only emerges after the "purely sensuous" has been repudiated through an act of the human will. It is created by the practice of virginity, the resistance to and separation from engulfment within the Mother. Because the ancient Hebrews were so successful at this practice of male virginity, ego consciousness emerged in its most highly developed form first among them. And, even today, only those adolescents who commit themselves to the practice of virginity for a significant period of time develop ego consciousness to a high degree. This is why, in our society, the adolescent boy separates himself from involvement with his mother and all touching and caressing, banding together with other boys in male groups (e.g. Scout troops and football teams) in order to develop his competence in courage and will. He is in the process of becoming an "I."

In tribal male groups, as in the modern Boy Scouts, men learn to control their sexual feelings, not by absolutely renouncing them, but by separating themselves from those people and situations that arouse them sexually. In this way, men "segment" their lives so that there are times and places where they do not feel the pull of instinctual sexuality. This segmentation extends even to their body feeling. One of the things that occur when ego consciousness evolves is that the human head takes over and rules the rest of the body. Through this ego organization of the body, sexual feelings—basic feelings of pleasure and pain—are delimited to certain parts of the body. In an infant, for example, the whole body is experienced as pleasurable; the whole body is experienced as libidinally arousing. But as ego consciousness emerges in the young boy, this body sensuality is more and more delimited, until it exists principally in his penis. This delimitation of sexual feeling is called "the genital organization of the body."

Here is one way this genital organization is learned. Many young boys play a game called "flinch." They take turns hitting, or pretending to hit, one another to see who is afraid. The boy who still experiences a high degree of sensitivity in the part of his body being hit is a sissy, a "mama's boy." He has not yet delimited his primal feelings of pleasure and pain within his body. His ego is not yet highly developed. He has not yet learned how to *segmentalize* his feelings. (It is, by the way, an evidence that we have less concern for developing ego consciousness in young girls that we do not encourage them to engage in such feats of voluntary courage. Rather, because we so often assume girls are to become solely wives and mothers, we try to limit their development of ego consciousness. For as wives and mothers, they identify themselves and live in terms of something and someone else. They are well suited to do this when mimetic consciousness remains dominant in them and they do not develop wills of their own.)

An interesting example of the success of the ancient Hebrews in segmentalizing sexual feeling and developing ego consciousness is seen in the story of Uriah, the husband of Bathsheba, the woman David took in adultery. "In the spring of the year, the time when the kings go forth to battle . . ." the Bible says, King David sent his army forth to fight in that traditional holy way that enhanced the power of the king and sacrificed a portion of the citizenry to the new social family, the city. Uriah was one of the soldiers.

We recall that in this ritual holy war, men were reconfirmed in the voluntary courage that is the foundation of the male group. During the time of this test, the men separated themselves from women, who aroused in them feelings of primal sexuality and weakness. In ancient Israel, this separation was officially required by ritual law, and it was because of this requirement that Uriah refused to sleep with his wife after David had called him back from the war in order to conceal the adultery. Uriah's refusal to break the code of the male group—in spite of the King's blandishments and urgings (not to mention Bathsheba's!)—is symbolic of the power of ego consciousness in ancient Israel.

If we compare, now, this strength of Uriah in fulfilling the requirements of voluntary courage with the utter failure of some contemporary Greeks—described in the farce *Lysistrata*—we see the significance of the biblical story. In this Greek comedy, we again see a male group engaged in that ritual war whose purpose it was to maintain the male's independence from and power over the female. The story of *Lysistrata* focuses upon the struggle for power between the two sexes. But in the Greek story the males lack the strength of Uriah. When the Greek women form a counterband of their own against the males and establish their own sexual independence, they destroy the male group, for the men have not yet learned how to do more than *temporarily* limit, or segment, their need for women. By their strategy, the Greek women force the men to relinquish power to them—or, more accurately, to share power with them. This is also the conclusion of Aeschylus' *Oresteia* trilogy, which ends with a compact reaffirming the ancient duality and coequality of the male and female principles. The failure of the Greek male group explains, in large part, the failure of the Greek cities to band themselves into a nation like that of the Israelites. And it explains, too, the failure of the Greeks to develop monotheism.

It might be objected that, in fact, the Greek *philosophers* did attain a conception of nationhood and the idea of a single cosmic principle. But the Greek philosophers did not reflect the views of Greek society at large. In Greek and Roman societies, the principle of "blood," the principle of ethnic loyalty and reverence for the Mother, was never totally eclipsed —neither by the patriarchal consciousness that triumphed in Israel nor by the mystical-philosophical consciousness that triumphed in Christianity. (Greek philosophy never formed the ethos of the Greek city; Greek philosophical consciousness only became dominant in Christianity.) For this reason, the position of women in Greek and Roman societies was always higher than the position of women in Hebrew society—and human sexuality was also "freer" in these societies. The price that was paid for this "freer" sexuality was a lesser development of ego consciousness and of human individuation.

CHAPTER III

Perpetual Virgins

The segmentalizing method of controlling sexuality assisted the development of ego consciousness in man. The possibility of this kind of sexual behavior arises out of and gives rise to the emerging ego. It eventuates in the genital organization of the human body. But, segmentalizing is not the sole method of sexual control and the genital organization of the body is not the sole alternative to the total sensuality ("polymorphous sexuality") of the infant's body feeling. The full evolution of human consciousness involves, as its concomitant, still other methods of sexual control and other possibilities for the sexual organization of body feeling.

The three methods of sexual control that will be considered in this book are (1) segmentalization, (2) renunciation, and (3) transformation. Just as the segmentalization of sexual behavior assists the development of ego consciousness, two other methods of sexual control give rise to characteristic kinds of consciousness. *The renunciation of instinctive sexuality is related to the evolutionary emergence of rational consciousness. The transformation of instinctive sexuality is related to the emergence of self-consciousness.* (I shall not, within this book, discuss those factors involved in the development of polyconsciousness, for this subject falls outside the range of questions that can be adequately discussed at this time.)

Moreover, just as there are three methods of sexual control, so there are appropriate institutions through which these methods of sexual control are learned. In the male group, men learn how to segmentalize sexual feeling. There is an institution analogous to the tribal male group that helps persons gain competence in the *renunciation* of instinctive sexuality. This institution is the noviceship, which provides training in asceticism. In the early Christian church the period of catechesis, when a man was preparing for confirmation, was such an institution teaching sexual asceticism. In the Middle Ages, the noviceship was conducted through the monasteries and the monastic schools.

In the same way, there is an institution in the modern world that teaches persons how to *transform* instinctual sexuality, to use sex as an instrument of interpersonal communion. This institution is *the age of adolescence,* which institutionalizes a "petting" process of ever-increasing personal-sexual intimacy within a heterosexual peer group.

I shall, in the pages that follow, fill out these highly abstract notions. But it may be helpful, at the present time, to map out their relations in a diagram. We use, as its basis, the several stages of evolution in human consciousness, adding to it (a) the three competences in sexual control and (b) the institutions through which these competences are learned.

STAGES OF CONSCIOUSNESS	METHOD OF CONTROL		INSTITUTION
1. mimetic consciousness			
2. ego consciousness	requires the	segmentalization of sex	which is learned in	the male group
3. rational consciousness	requires the	renunciation of sex	which is learned in	monastic traini
4. self-consciousness	requires the	transformation of sex	which is learned in	adolescent petti

Just as the male group developed a competence in maintaining an ego consciousness that was the foundation of legal-covenantal (or "kingship") society, so the classical philosophical and monastic exercises in asceticism developed a competence in rational consciousness that was the foundation of yet another social vision. We have seen that kingship and the city are expressions of ego consciousness, built on the legal-monarchical will, and engaging in a characteristic sacrificial ritual: the holy war. We shall see in what follows that rational consciousness is expressed in a social vision that goes beyond the ideal of the city (or "nation"). Rational consciousness gives rise to the social ideal of an absolutely universal community, of a mankind that is *one spiritual family*. (Biological families and legal-covenantal cities can never conceive themselves to be universal. Particularity is of their essence. To conceive, therefore, of a universal community that is a single family of man is to conceive of man and his "sexual love" in a nonbiological way.)

The leader of this new universal community must, of course, be quite different from the king who rules over a legal-covenantal society. The leader of a universal community will rule not by will (the power of ego), but by wisdom (the power of reason). The "king" of a universal community, or spiritual family, must be a "philosopher" (Plato) or an incarnation, or avatar, of Truth (Buddhism, the Gospel of John). He must rule over men in a way other than the way Caesars rule. He must rule in a way that confounds monarchical kingship in order to make clear that his kingdom is not of this earth—with all its ethnic partialities rooted in biological limitation or human might. He must rule as a "servant" (the Synoptic Gospels). He must form his new universal community not through the power of his ego and his will, but through the power of his knowledge and understanding. For the universal community of mankind arises out of the recognition that all men are essentially one—that neither ethnicity, nor sexuality, nor social condition defines man as he essentially is. Neither Greek nor Jew, nor bond nor free, nor male nor female has anything to do with man's destiny and what he should know himself to be.

For a man to attain to a consciousness of himself as a being whose social fulfillment is in a universal community or spiritual family requires that he evolve beyond ego consciousness. And this evolution necessarily includes a new way of ordering his sexual behavior. For, to recall our axiom, every awareness includes a self-awareness. And every self-awareness includes some sense of what man's sexual potentialities might be.

The historical emergence of rational consciousness occurred between 800 and 400 b.c., not simply in one part of the world, but in many different places. The Buddha, Zoroaster, the Hebrew prophets, the Greek philosophers—all emerged within this period. The conception of reality held by these figures broke completely with what had gone before. It was as if—to use Plato's image—all men before them had been enclosed in a dark cave.

What was the new thing that these men saw? They all became aware of a Transcendent Immutable Reality. They suddenly experienced that there was, behind the human will as well as behind the biological processes of birth and change and death, a changeless world. There was a higher kind of Life above and beyond the life of nature and history. There was a Life that was not subject to mutability and death and decay, a Life whose structure and order pervaded every biological and historical entity and caused them to be alive. Men experienced this Transcendent Life as Spirit, Eternal Reason, Unchangeable Truth.

So remarkable is this new evolution of consciousness, and so pervasive have been its consequences for all later generations, that this moment in history has been called the axial period. The whole of modern science as well as all universal religions begin with, and build on, its vision. What men realized in this moment is that the world of change is not ultimately explainable in terms of itself. Rather, they saw that the order of change manifests a changeless order. It expresses, through its mutability, the power of immutability. In other words, men saw all change has a rational structure that does not change, but is that changeless thing in terms of which we understand the changing. The changing world, from this moment on, is contrasted with the rational world. The world of sensory experience and volition is contrasted with the world of rational "abstraction." The realm of human action and passion is contrasted with the realm of human contemplation—for a man does not *interact* with the Eternal, but can only contemplate it through an act of rational understanding.

In the axial period man became aware that there are two kinds of life. There is a life that is linked with change and death, and there is a higher rational life that is not limited or qualified by death. There is a life that is part of the process of life and death, and there is a life that is All Life. The first of these is temporal; the second is spiritual. To become aware of this Life that is Eternal Spirit requires the presence of a new kind of consciousness in man. We have seen that the emergence of ego consciousness occurred when man defined himself in terms of his volition, his active power to command and to obey. But the human will is not adequate to raise man's consciousness to an intellectual vision of Transcendent Eternal Truth. For a man to know this Unchanging Order, a new capacity must emerge within his own consciousness: man's capacity to withhold himself from action in order to contemplate and simply view. Today we call man's capacity to purge himself of passions and volitions in order to contemplate something "objectively" man's reason. Man's reason is his capacity not to will, but *to know in a theoretical, or purely contemplative, way*. The evolution of this rational consciousness displaces the will from its central, or organizing, place in man's life and replaces it with *reason*.

[Those who find themselves put off by the notion of an Unchanging or Transcendent dimension of Reality should note that it is not the truth of such a notion that is essential to my argument. What we are concerned with is the evolution of human consciousness and sexual behavior. Therefore, it makes no difference to my argument whether or not an Unchanging or Transcendent Reality truly exists. All that is important is that man, beginning at this axial period, experienced something that he called an Eternal World. That he felt himself as experiencing such a thing is a fact of history, not theology. And this historical fact is not in dispute. The theological question whether early man was right in his judgment that there is an Eternal Reality is beside the point. For what is at stake here is merely that he conceived that there was such a Reality and, in so conceiving, became aware of a new kind of consciousness within himself.]

When man became rationally conscious, defining himself in terms of the centrality and priority of his reason, he became a new kind of man. He no longer thought of himself as a being defined in terms of ethnicity, social class, and sex. He thought of himself "abstractly," that is, in universal terms.

Rational consciousness *universalizes.* Through rational consciousness, a man becomes aware that the particular limitations that define his ethnic and sexual and social situation do not determine who he is. Such limitations are but appearance, or illusion; for behind the life that is history there is an immutable, spiritual life in which man participates. And it is man's participation in this unchanging and all-pervading spiritual life that defines for the rationally conscious man what he feels he essentially is. *He identifies with what is universal and eternally true.*

Before considering how, in the axial period, men gave up their particular ego consciousnesses and identified themselves with what is universal, let us first take an example of such a stage in the psychological development of an American adolescent. The key to rational consciousness is the development of the power of abstract thinking. This is why, Plato noted, the study of mathematics, logic, and harmonics assists its growth. Rational consciousness is awareness of that which is universal; what is universal is first sensed as something abstract.

If we consider the process of psychological development, we see that today the capacity to think in abstractions and universals (something different from thinking abstractly through metaphors, which even a child can do) emerges at adolescence. The child thinks in terms of particulars, but an adolescent begins to think in terms of abstractions. He begins to think about the "big" questions—: whether there is a God, whether life is good, whether the social system is corrupt, what it is to be a man. These questions are abstract. They are questions about the universality of being. And to ask such questions, to attain to rational consciousness, is characteristic of the adolescent stage of life.

An adolescent begins to think abstractly long before rational, or universal, consciousness becomes the dominant and defining characteristic of his life. But notice that as the adolescent becomes older, this rational consciousness grows in strength until it becomes the awareness that organizes all his other perceptions—until it becomes the dominant awareness that includes a new kind of *self-awareness*. When an adolescent moves toward his late teens or early twenties, he frequently becomes so rational that he seeks to redefine himself in totally universal terms.

Consider, for example, how today the adolescent Marxist or Christian or hippie-Buddhist experiences his world. He experiences it in terms of an ideology, an abstract system of doctrine that he believes explains—or explains away—everything in his sensory ego experience. The young Marxist is convinced that no matter how seriously politicians and businessmen seek to improve the world, they are "capitalist exploiters." The fundamentalist Christian knows that no matter how decent and moral nonreligious people are, they are sinful and going to hell. On the basis of their ideological consciousness, their convictions that they know an immutable and universal truth that governs all things, young adolescents will not accept their ordinary, sensible experiences. These experiences belong to a world of changing "appearance" that for them is neither true nor ultimately real. What is real for the ideologist is a universal, abstract truth.

I am not saying here that the ideological consciousness of the modern adolescent is the same thing as the philosophical consciousness of Plato or Jesus or of the Buddha. What I want to point out is that ideological consciousness is one form of rational consciousness. A person cannot think ideologically or philosophically or theologically unless he can think abstractly and in universal terms. The emergence of this capacity to think in universal terms is the emergence of rational consciousness.

It will help, moreover, if we now go on to consider how the emergence of this rational consciousness in an adolescent affects his self-image and his behavior (recalling our axiom that every consciousness includes a specific self-awareness). We all experience how an adolescent, in whom ideological consciousness has come to full dominance, begins to think of himself in a new way and to behave differently. He ceases to act like an ego with private desires and he tries to universalize himself. He tries to live abstractly, as the embodiment of his universal truth. He tries to be an individual instance of the rational truth, or nature, that he is conscious of. He lives, breathes, eats, talks, and sleeps "Marxism" or "Christianity" or some other "ism." And he submits his sexual life and his personal desires to this truth and the success of his Cause. This frequently means that he accepts some form of sexual self-denial for the sake of his doctrine. The fervent Christian will remain chaste because he believes in the Christian doctrine of exclusive love. The young Marxist will renounce private sexual relations as a distraction from the demands of the revolution. (The sexually integrated Viet Cong troops do not apparently have much trouble with fornication!)

We have all known people who think of themselves and live this way. To be a Marxist, or a doctrinaire Christian, or a committed Women's Liberationist means to identify oneself with a universal Truth and cause. Through such an act, a person attains an abstract identity. He sacrifices all the peculiarities and idiosyncrasies of his ego to his universal truth. For he no longer believes that his individual ego with all its idiosyncrasies and desires is of first importance. He sacrifices these in order that the new man—and the new social community that seems to express his rational consciousness—may come into being.

Just as we saw that mimetic man sacrificed himself in actual immolation so that the cycle of nature might continue, and that ego conscious man sacrificed himself in holy war so that the new social unit—the city —might come into existence, so we see that rational man will sacrifice even his sexual life in order to manifest and bring into existence a universal community of men who are bound together through their affirmation of an abstract ideology. This new community of men who live by wisdom, by their knowledge of a truth that is universal, is most accurately called a "holy catholic church." I do not mean, of course, that Communists, Buddhists, Christians, and all other ideologists believe in the Christian church. What I am saying is that the notion of an invisible, universal, and holy (or ultimate) community of all mankind is implied in the notion of rational consciousness itself. The Marxist believes, of course, that this ultimate community will be a Marxist utopia; the Christian believes it will be a Christian utopia. Both of these notions are structurally similar. They are both examples of a new social ideal: the ideal of a universal community of all mankind, created by the renunciation of the limiting relationships established through the biological family. Just as mimetic consciousness found expression in the tribe and just as ego consciousness found expression in the city, so rational consciousness finds its social exemplification in the ideal of a universal community of mankind.

The reason for discussing the modern adolescent's desire to identify himself with an abstract ideology—and all that this involves with respect to the sacrifice of his concrete individuality—is that it shows a parallel in the psychological order to what took place when human rational consciousness first emerged in the axial period of history (800–400 b.c.). In this historical moment, man first became aware of an all-pervasive rational principle by which everything else was governed. He renounced his private preferences and volitions in order to be an incarnation of this abstract truth. This is, after all, why Socrates chose to be put to death unjustly rather than to save his life by fleeing. It was a matter of principle. This is why Jesus chose to sacrifice himself to "doing the will of his Father." The emergence of rational consciousness in a man leads him to live as an individual embodiment of reason itself. So the early Christian definition of man stated that "a person is an individual substance of a rational nature." Whatever about man does not manifest the universality of "rational nature" is to be renounced or suppressed as mere appearance, a nonessential aspect of his life.

It was in early Christianity that this new rational consciousness came to its fullest expression, permeating and becoming the controlling factor in the new community. In conjunction with this new consciousness, there also emerged novel possibilities for human sexuality. The most radical of Christianity's sexual innovations was the practice of perpetual virginity, the significance of which has not been sufficiently explained in evolutionary terms. What will concern us here, therefore, is the impact of Christian virginity upon the evolution of human consciousness.

Perpetual virginity involves the absolute renunciation, not the mere segmentalization, of the desire for sexual intercourse. Even to imagine the possibility that sexual desire can be renounced involves the presence of a new kind of human consciousness, a consciousness wherein a man no longer identifies with and feels the instinctual sexuality of his body as truly his own. Perpetual virginity is possible only for those who know themselves not simply as embodied "egos," but as individuals who participate in the unchanging immortal and universal spirit. Persons who identify with this immortal spirit do not feel that their own destinies, their own immortality, are tied up with having children who will continue to bear their name and keep their ethnic group alive. (This new feeling can be seen in the *Symposium,* for example, where Plato suggests that the desire of time-bound men for biological progeny is but a lower-grade manifestation of the same desire for immortality that appears in wise men as the desire for eternal life.) Note the shift that has occurred. Whereas the prerational man found his "immortality" and genuine happiness through his family and children, the rational man finds his fulfillment through a union with an eternal transcendent order—hence, sex is accidental rather than essential to his life.

Once man realizes that true life is found through wisdom, he no longer believes his fulfillment is in his patriarchal rule over a family and the fathering of biological descendants who shall number a great clan—a notion that makes sex *essential* to human fulfillment. Rather, his fulfillment is now the *visio dei,* that "wisdom" concerning eternal things for whose sake a man renounces desire for the pleasures of this world—including a wife, sexual pleasure, and progeny.

After this axial transition, the ancient male group (which inculcated that sense of male dominance over women necessary for a legal-covenantal society) was replaced by the esoteric spiritual community (the philosopher's school, the Essene sect, the Gnostic cult, the early Christian *koinonia,* and the monasteries).

[Since the historical unit utilized in this analysis is the *axial epoch,* we are overlooking the obvious differences among the several *historical periods* that all belong within the same *axial epoch*. There is, of course, a difference among the sexual ideals and behavior characteristic of the Hellenistic, early Christian, and medieval periods of history—just as there is a difference among the philosophers' schools, the gnostic sects, the early Christian *koinonia*, and the monasteries. But it is no less important to note that in all these periods of history that fall within the same *axial epoch*, the renunciation of coitus is highly valued.]

The exercises of this esoteric spiritual community helped men develop a sense of the unchanging transcendent world and to renounce altogether the world of flesh, mortality, and change. Such a *renunciation* of instinctive sexual behavior is altogether different from the *segmentation* of this behavior from personal, voluntary activity that was inculcated by the male groups. Moreover, such a renunciation also implies that in post-axial cultures (where the male group is replaced by the spiritual novitiate), the primacy of the family is also displaced. For a man's happiness and destiny are now seen to be functions of the religious community of saints; while the biological family, with its procreational function, is ultimately incompatible with this. The incompatibility between the bio-logical-procreational family and the new universal community arises from the fact that the biological family institutionalizes degrees of distance among persons. Some are felt to be "closer" to you than others. The expression of this institutionalization of degrees of closeness is private property. The biological family seeks, first of all, to take care of its own members. It justifies the distinction between mine and thine. It teaches men that they are not as responsible for some human beings as they are for others. The biological family is not simply the symbol, but the very cause, of the conviction that all men are not brothers. The responsible family man cannot, in all his dealings, be a good Samaritan. This is why the biological family is ultimately incompatible with the ideal of the universal family of man.

The commitment to perpetual virginity, therefore, is not simply a visible symbol that what is ultimately real is an unchanging spiritual order. It is also a way of regulating human sexuality so that the universal family of man might come into being. The renunciation of sexual inter-course is not the renunciation of love. It is, rather, the renunciation of that kind of love that has sexual orgasm and procreation as its purpose. The renunciation of sexual intercourse—i.e., the commitment to perpetual virginity—means that man now loves in a different way. The purpose of his love ceases to be procreation and the establishment of a family and becomes caritas, the love of the soul in the body.

As long as men and women think of themselves exclusively as bodies and in terms of biological functions, they assume that no individual man or individual woman is a complete person. Each is regarded as incomplete in himself, and only as a man and a woman are joined sexually are they "one flesh," or one complete (androgynous) being. This is the pre-axial point of view. It regards sexual union as the sole possible method of becoming a complete person: a man knows himself only from sexual union with a woman, and vice versa. But this is precisely why the ancient world believed that a personal, voluntary *friendship* between a man and a woman was impossible; men and women were assumed to be different kinds of beings. They could be related to each other only *sexually,* not by the moral communion of friendship—for friendship presupposes full equality and likeness of humanity in each of the persons united in this moral communion.

Friendship is not the sexual completion of the humanity of one person by another as the two reform themselves into the original androgyne ("one flesh"); rather, it is a moral and spiritual communion between two beings, each of whom is generically complete in himself because the fullness of "human-beingness" is present in each individual person. The classical Christian definition of a person shows this: a person is "an individual being with a rational nature." This means that a man does not need a woman to complete him, and vice versa. Each is a complete human being by himself alone.

Precisely because the age following the first axial transition encouraged the awareness of a spiritual essence of man that transcends the body by being related to the eternal and unchanging (the *nous,* the Creator, the Spirit of Christ), it opened the way to the new possibility of moral communion, or friendship, between men and women. For as the realization grew that rational and moral power is not limited to men alone, and that women also have a soul as well as a body, the character of spiritual love as *transsexual* was more fully understood.

[The patriarchal assumption was, of course, that women possess less rational-moral power and are more determined by the sexuality of their bodies than are men. Even today we reiterate such a prejudice when we assert that men are fulfilled through their work, but women through their children. Such an assertion presupposes that sexuality is less important for a man than it is for a woman. The reason for drawing attention to this patriarchal supposition is that it allows us to understand why, following the emergence of Christianity, virginity comes to be understood primarily as a female achievement (thus *reversing* the presupposition of pre-axial history). For if, assuming the patriarchal point of view, only the female is really sexual, then virginity—or the total renunciation of all sexual activity—is heroic, or counter-natural, only in *her*. In order, therefore, for the character of transsexual or spiritual love to be fully affirmed, it required not the virginity of a male, but the virginity of a female. The archetype of this virginity is Mary, the model of all Christian nuns. She, with them, is the virgin who brings the Eternal Truth and who manifests the spiritual possibilities open to all men and women.]

The idea of a transsexual, or spiritual, love between a man and a woman is hard for our own age to entertain. We can therefore appreciate its strangeness to the world two thousand years ago. Yet so powerful was the new experience of the spirit and the taste of transsexual, or spiritual, love that in early Christianity the commitment to permanent virginity as the basis for a truly spiritual marriage became a not uncommon practice. As D. S. Bailey observes,

"The most remarkable manifestation of sexual asceticism in the early Church was undoubtedly the phenomenon known as syneisaktism, or spiritual marriage —that is, a cohabitation of the sexes under conditions of strict continence, a couple sharing the same house, often the same room, and sometimes even the same bed, yet conducting themselves as brother and sister. . . . Certain of the solitary ascetics of the desert were accompanied each by a female hermit who acted more or less as a maidservant to the holy man; in the ancient Irish Church monks and nuns lived together in monastic establishments; and in towns and cities women shared the dwellings of priests, and even of bishops, as housekeepers or spiritual companions."[8]

Soon monasteries, some including the chaste cohabitation of men and women working and praying together, grew up as an institutional response to the new understanding of a nonsexual, spiritual love. In such religious communities, there was full equality between men and women, and occasionally even the rule of a prioress over mixed houses. Intimations of such a development already appear in the New Testament. Virginity, or the absolute renunciation of sexual intercourse, opened the way to this new kind of spiritual community and to the new kind of full equality of men and women that it involved. It opened the way, moreover, to a new kind of love between men and women: personal love, the love of friendship, the love of contemplative enjoyment of one another that exists for its own sake. Those who experienced—and still experience—this spiritual love know by how much it exceeds the joys of sexual intercourse.

Once the reality of this spiritual love has been experienced, it is possible to ask whether sexual intercourse itself might be so transformed and elevated that it can be integrated within it. And this is, in fact, what occurs in the next evolutionary stage. But the first experience of this spiritual love between man and woman was so startling and so satisfying that for a thousand years the practice of perpetual virginity was joyously chosen as the way to love more fully. This virginity was not the repudiation, but the enhancement, of love and the dignity of both man and woman.

Part Two

THE WITCH

CHAPTER IV

"All Men Are Animals"

WE turn now to the evolution of human consciousness and sexuality within a third historical epoch: modern technological culture. Since the tendencies characteristic of modern technology are most developed in America, we shall focus on this society in developing the issues at stake. It is important to realize, however, that these modern tendencies are also found in other societies. In fact, were it not for the greater diversity and ethnicity of Great Britain, it would perhaps have been more accurate to choose this society as the paradigm.

The evolution of modern culture follows a *second* axial transition, a transition no less in magnitude than the *first*. At the first axial transition, the consciousness of an unchanging transcendent order emerged and was the basis for the reorganization of human life, including sexual behavior. At the second axial transition, man conceived the idea that he himself might recreate the world of nature to accord with a vision of his own imagination. In such a world all things would be artificial (i.e., products of man's technical reason) and symbolic (i.e., visible presentations of ideas first existing in the human imagination). This artificial and sym-

bolic world, recreated by the power of the human imagination, would also be totally moralized and rationalized. It would be rationalized since whatever is recreated by man is reordered by the requirements of human reason and remade to suit man's scale. Such a reordering of the world to express the capacities and reason of man was the vision behind Renaissance humanism.

In this modern vision, the desires of man and the potentialities of nature are believed to be perfectly congruent. Man no longer believes there is any instinctual realm excluded from this recreated world to which he must still *submit*. Rather, he believes that nature and spirit can be reconciled. He believes that nature can be transformed to express the full rationality of man's own mind and to allow man to attain, within nature, all his own purposes. The belief in the transformability of nature is the foundation of modern technology.

But the belief that nature can be transformed includes, at least implicitly, the belief that man's own nature can be transformed. It includes man's conviction that he can modify his own desires. For as man reconstructs his world, he also reconstructs himself. The project of technology includes the transformation of man. One of the things reconstructed by man in the modern period is his own sexual feelings and behavior. Just as man breaks down physical nature into atoms in order to reconstitute synthetic materials and artificial forms, so he also now begins to break down his instinctual drives into their constituent parts in order to construct new behavioral possibilities for himself.

What is the foundation in human consciousness for man's idea that he might transform himself? What is the foundation in human consciousness that allows man to think of himself as an object for himself? For, as I have maintained throughout this book, every consciousness implies a determinate self-awareness in man. The counterpart of the consciousness that he is able to transform his world includes, necessarily, some evolution in man's own consciousness of himself. This modern evolution of man's consciousness is his coming to *self-consciousness*.

In discussing the first axial transition (eighth to fourth centuries b.c.) we saw that a distinctive evolution in human self-awareness took place, namely, the evolution in man of *rational consciousness.* And we saw that, through this rational consciousness, man undertook to universalize himself, to live as an individual in whom theoretical or abstract reason comes to perfect expression. At the second axial transition, a transition occurring between the thirteenth and seventeenth centuries a.d., a further complexification of human consciousness takes place. Man becomes *self-conscious.* He begins to reflect upon his own consciousness and to become aware of *himself* as its free and active cause. By man's reflection on his own consciousness and on himself as its cause, man creates a subject-object polarity *within himself.* He begins to experience his own consciousness. It is this experience of duality within his own consciousness that constitutes man's *self*-consciousness. It is this experience of duality that allows man to think of himself as an object for himself.

The duality in man's consciousness of himself is what underlies man's imaginative conception that he might transform both nature and human nature. For man to conceive the possibility of transforming the world outside him necessarily implies that man imagines himself capable of changing himself. For when man imagines his world might be different, he must also imagine himself as capable of being different. The possibility of man's imagining himself as different—of imagining that he might feel, experience, and behave differently—presupposes his capacity to regard himself as an "object" for himself. It presupposes that man's consciousness be "*self*-conscious."

The polarity within a self that is *self*-conscious allows a man to reflect upon and objectify his own drives, feelings, and behavior. This preliminary objectification of himself to himself creates an inner space and fulcrum from which man may get a certain leverage on his own behavior. It allows him to experiment with his drives and feelings. It allows him to apply behavioral technology to himself so that he may change the pattern of his own inner and outer life. Such a change, enhancing the development of self-consciousness, is presupposed by psychoanalysis. For example, through the psychoanalytic process, by which a person learns to objectify his feelings and behavior, a process of gradually transforming the self is begun. But most important of all of the transformations of human behavior implicit in the evolution of self-consciousness is the transformation of the human *"instincts."* Through heightened self-consciousness, a man is able to overcome their relative autonomy from the conscious self-system and bring them within its purview and intentions. Man is able to rationalize, moralize, and personalize his own instinctual drives. This is the first consequence of the evolution of self-consciousness.

There is a second concomitant to the development of self-consciousness that is also decisive for the evolution of human sexuality in modern times. Just as the inner "space" created in the self-conscious self allows a man to objectify and transform his instinctual drives and feelings, so this same inner self-self polarity also allows a man to have a new experience of what a personal relation is. Before self-consciousness is developed, a man never knows within himself what a personal relation is. Another person always appears to be outside and over-against him exactly as a stone is outside and over-against him. As such, a man always experiences and thinks of persons impersonally. He thinks of them as objects. He does not realize that personal relationships are not like relations between persons and things—for persons can, so to say, enter into one another and know one another *from inside out.* This is one of the things that happens when people learn how to tell one another how they feel, how the world appears to them, how the other person is affecting them. Through personal talking with one another, persons learn to experience one another from *the other's point of view.* They learn what it actually means to say that man is not a thing, but a spiritual being who can be related internally to another spiritual being. They learn from experience what an "intimate relation" is. For only spiritual beings, beings able to reproduce themselves within others by the power of personal conversation, are able to be related internally and intimately.

The desire for such intimate relation, as the highest form of love, arises only in the modern world. Such an ideal presupposes the evolution of self-consciousness in man. For a man to experience another person from that person's own point of view, for him to have highly developed capacities for empathy, requires that he be able to separate himself from himself and identify with that other. Such an act of empathetic identification with another presupposes a highly developed self-consciousness. For in the act of identifying with another, a person separates himself from himself. He gives up his own feeling and point of view in order to experience another's. Only persons who have first learned how to make this distinction of self from self within themselves are able to identify with others. Only those who are self-conscious are capable of experiencing themselves both as themselves and "another," both as another and "themselves."

The transformation of human sexuality following the emergence of self-consciousness in man requires two things: first, the actual integration of the sexual drive within the totality of voluntary personality—that is, the unification of sex and love; second, the creation of a new psychological relationship between men and women within which this new "sexual love" can find expression and fulfillment.

It is extremely difficult for Americans today to realize that what they accept as the normal sexual ideal—that is, the unity of sex and love— is a relatively recent phenomenon. That such a unity of sex and love could even be *imagined* as a possibility is a tremendous cultural achievement. To imagine the possibility of sexual love itself is the evidence of man's new self-image. *Self-consciousness* contains within itself the new image of man as a being who can unify within himself the voluntary and the instinctual, the sexual and the sublime.

The reason why it has only been possible in modern times to imagine that sex and love can be combined is that the sexual drive toward orgasm (hereafter to be called the "genital drive") emerges in the lives of people at the age of puberty, that is, at an age when their voluntary personalities are already to a large degree formed. When this genital drive develops, it is experienced as an instinctual mechanism having an autonomous character of its own. The key to the notion of an instinct is this autonomous mechanism. It operates, at least in the beginning, whether we are conscious of it and whether we are willing for it to operate or not. An instinct is, therefore, different from a human volition. One can freely choose not to eat, but one cannot keep from feeling hungry. One can freely choose not to have sexual relations, but one cannot keep from having sexual feelings. Instincts seem to be powers that operate in man separate from and free from the control of the human will.

The genital drive, or sexual instinct, seems, however, to be an especially "autonomous mechanism." This is because the genital drive emerges in persons *after* their voluntary personalities are formed. The genital drive seems suddenly to erupt at puberty as a strange and foreign power operating inside one's body, as a tendency toward inner division, as a threat to the voluntary control over oneself that has been so laboriously constructed in the first twelve years of one's life. When, for example, one lives with young teenage boys and girls and sees how the emergence of sexual feeling in them disrupts their ordinary patterns of behavior and, in a sense, forces them back upon themselves to find ways of coping with this new inner development, then one is struck by the strong power of the genital drive when it first emerges.

Notice that the emergence of the genital drive is unlike the emergence of the other primary instinctual drives in that it comes forth after the voluntary personality of an individual has been formed to a greater or lesser degree. The other instinctual needs—the need for food and oral gratification, the need for control over the movements of one's body—these all are operative in man from infancy. They *predate* the existence of voluntary personality and, in fact, the emergence of freedom and consciousness in man requires that a degree of voluntary control over these instinctual drives be established. Once this is done, a man no longer experiences his eating and his defecation as purely instinctual mechanisms that operate without any self-consciousness or choice. In the very formation of his consciousness, he has transformed them so that they are integrated within the range of his freedom. Moreover, since a man's conscious memory exists only from the time that his consciousness itself has been integrated and formed (hence, we do not remember our own birth because there was no conscious power of memory in us at birth), we never consciously experience our needs for food or for bowel control as "instinctual mechanisms having a total autonomy of their own."

The situation is different with regard to the genital drive, however. This drive emerges after the human personality and human freedom have been developed. It is therefore experienced as a threat to them, as an autonomous mechanism that has not been—like the other basic human drives—worked into the unity of the whole person. If the genital drive and voluntary-personal actions are to be unified, so that sex can become an expression of love, the structure of human personality must be kept open for a period of time during puberty so that the same kind of integration of instinct and volition that men learn in relation to eating can also be learned with respect to sexual behavior. Persons must learn "sexual control" in the same way that infants learn to control their appetites.

But precisely because the human personality has already attained to a degree of stability at the age of puberty, there are many different ways of harmonizing the genital drive with the personal-voluntary aspects of human love. For example, it is possible to harmonize them by separating them rather than unifying them. In ancient Greek, as in modern Japanese, society, the way of harmonizing the two drives was to keep them focused on different persons, or objects. The drive for orgasm and procreation was institutionalized within marriage and focused on the wife while the unitive drive for love and friendship was institutionalized within homosexual groups, or carried over into love-relationships with the geisha, courtesan, or mistress. This way of harmonizing the two drives, by keeping them separate, is consistent with the need to establish an order within the personality. It accepts, however, a higher degree of autonomy for the genital drive than Americans today find acceptable.

A second way of harmonizing the two drives is to direct them at the same person, but allow them to remain separate and unreconciled. In this situation, a man may love his wife and also have sexual intercourse with her—but the intercourse is not intended or experienced as an expression of love. For example, a southern lady of my acquaintance, in commenting on the total happiness of her marriage with her husband—a relationship that seemed to be governed by ever-growing love—added, as an afterthought, "Of course, all men are just animals in bed." What she was saying is that the sexual life between her husband and herself had never been brought within the range of acts expressive of voluntary *love*. She loved her husband, recognized that he had sexual needs, and was willing to quiet those needs. But it never occurred to her, or to him, that sexual intercourse could be raised from the "need level" to the voluntary "love level" of life. In such a relationship, the harmony between love and sex is maintained by recognizing the totally instinctual character of the sexual drive and *segmenting* it off into particular times and places. Hence, for example, it was common for Victorian husbands and wives never to express sexual affection to one another outside the bedroom— or for the husband never to see his wife's naked body. In the darkened bedroom he might touch it, but that relationship was relatively anonymous and as separate from their personal relationship as night from day.

A third way of harmonizing the two drives is, of course, to renounce sex altogether (as in monasticism). In fact, without at least a temporary renunciation of sex as a way of gaining full power of negation over sexual behavior, there is no way to move on to the fourth way of harmonizing the two drives by unifying them completely with one another. The modern ideal of the unity of sex and love actually presupposes the psychological capacities that were first developed through the institution of perpetual virginity and monasticism.

The fourth way of unifying the genital drive with the totality of rational-volitional consciousness is to transform that drive so that it operates only within the range of voluntary love. Such a transformation means, of course, that one only has sexual desire for a person whom one loves. It means that sexual desire is no longer experienced as an anonymous generalized drive looking for release (Kinsey's "outlets"), but is experienced rather as a possibility for physical intimacy that is created by the presence of the beloved. It means that where there is no love, there is no sexual desire—where the beloved is absent, there is no desire for intercourse. It means that love creates the condition or possibility for sex. It means that every act of sexual intercourse is an act of *genital love*.

Where the experience of genital love, or the total integration of sex and love, has been developed, every sexual act now aims not at private satisfaction (i.e., orgasm), but at personal communion with another. This is because the genital drive toward orgasm no longer operates independently of the communitive, or love, drive. Once sex no longer exists as an end in itself, but as a means of communication and intimate sharing, the goal of sex is mutuality and union. This explains why the ideal of simultaneous orgasm emerges. In America—and only in America—is the goal of simultaneous orgasm thought to be the ideal fulfillment of the sexual relation. What this concept is trying to express is that what makes sex satisfactory is not the orgasm itself, but the simultaneity or perfect mutuality of the persons who unite themselves to one another through the act of sexual love.

In America today, where the ideal of the unity of sex and love is so widely held, it is quite consistent that purely private orgasm (or sexual intercourse for the sake of orgasm alone) is not experienced as satisfactory. What Americans want in sex, and quite rightly, is not orgasm, but orgasm *à deux*. To attain this goal requires, of course, a new psychological relation between men and women. It requires that in the act of intercourse they not be anonymous ("animals"), but participate in one another's feelings and desires. Only to the extent that they do this, coordinating their personal-sexual feelings and behavior, can they attain to communitive pleasure—which is the kind of sexual pleasure characteristic of the *self-conscious* human being.

Such an experience of genital love is only possible, of course, for persons who have managed to integrate in a total way their genital and their personal life. That much literature on human sexuality assumes that such an integration of personal and sexual feeling is impossible reveals more about the experience of those who write such books than it does about possibilities for human sexual life. In persons who have, however, attained a certain level of psychosexual integration, genital feeling is aroused only in conjunction with particular beloved persons and the primary satisfaction gained from sexual intercourse is not orgasm, but communion.

The unification, or total integration, of genital and personal feeling cannot occur, of course, without the exercise of the human will. For this reason, says Michael Balint, "what we call *genital love* is as much a creation of human culture as is art or religion."[9] But though it is a cultural achievement, *genital love* is no less natural than allowing the genital and volitional dimensions of man to remain separate. In fact, once this cultural achievement becomes "normal," it is no less a cultural (or "artificial") achievement to reseparate the human instincts and the human volition once again, restoring the primal autonomy of the genital drive. When, for example, Masters and Johnson *reteach* the genital drive to operate as an autonomous mechanism that strives toward private orgasm, they are not restoring "natural sexuality," but are creating an alternative cultural solution to the problem of harmonizing human volition and sexual appetition. In a self-conscious society, such "spontaneous sexuality" is no less a willed achievement than is the full integration of the instinctual drives within the self-conscious control of a person.

It is important to realize that the rhetoric of "spontaneous sex" and "sexual freedom" always involves some decision about how man is to come to terms with his instinctual drives. For example, if one regards all attempts to renounce or transform the genital drive as impossible in principle, then every attempt to do so will be called "repression"—and the only way that man will be said to be perfectly free is if he allows his instinctual drives to operate in their primitive autonomous manner. Those who hold this view will regard man's true freedom as *instinctual freedom*—freedom for man's instinctual nature to operate without the interference of his conscious will.

On the other hand, if a man experiences the possibility of renouncing, but not transforming, genital sexuality, then he will regard man's true freedom as *ascetical freedom*. This is the traditional view of the Roman Catholic Church—which questions the possibility of transforming and fully integrating the genital drive within the range of personal volition and love, but affirms the possibility of renouncing this drive through the vow of chastity. Through chastity, man becomes *ascetically free*—which on the traditional Catholic view is man's only true freedom. Ascetical freedom copes with all threats to human volition and consciousness by withdrawing from, or renouncing, those things that could limit them.

The third form of freedom—full voluntary, or personal, freedom—involves man's becoming self-conscious about his genital sexuality and his gradually learning to overcome its original instinctual autonomy. Through the process of sexual learning, he gradually learns to extend the scope of his freedom over his own sexuality, finally personalizing it. He attains power over instinctual mechanisms that, when they first appeared, had power over him. This third kind of freedom is a radically different conception of how man is related to his biological drives than either instinctual freedom or ascetical freedom. Such a vision of enhancing man's freedom in this way is uniquely modern and, strictly speaking, is the dominant ideal only in modern times—and especially in America.

[While Europe has modernized in many ways, the characteristic European view of nature is still pre-modern. Europeans tend to assume that nature is an autonomous mechanism to which men must adjust. Hence, the Freudian calls all attempts at the personalization of sex "repression." Herbert Marcuse attacks Norman Brown's vision of LOVE'S BODY "unrealistic." Konrad Lorenz argues that aggression is an instinctual mechanism that must be allowed to operate—since it cannot be suppressed. The Nazis argued that the consciousness of every man was really a function of the soil and landscape of his nation. Even the Pope speaks of sexual intercourse as having its own intrinsic biological purpose—a purpose that must be allowed to operate autonomously. We see, in these various judgments, that the European view of nature assumes it is an autonomous, self-contained mechanism.]

CHAPTER V

Lady or Witch

THE question we turn to now is, "How is this new integrated psychosexual behavior learned?" The mere emergence of self-consciousness in man creates the possibility of man's imagining that he might transform his own instinctual drives, integrating them within the unity of his voluntary life. It creates the possibility for man's imagining a new kind of intimacy —for through self-consciousness he learns what it feels like to be "psychologically inside" another person. But it is one thing to imagine a new possibility and it is something else to learn how to realize that possibility in actual life. Not only, therefore, did self-consciousness have to emerge, but there had to be someone to work out—experimentally—what this new consciousness implied for human sexual life. The great experimenters, the persons who dared invent a whole new form of sexual interaction, were a relatively small number of late medieval aristocrats who invented what we today call "courtly love."

What the courtly lovers aimed to do was totally personalize and voluntarize sexual feeling and behavior. They set out to bring man's sexual drives within the range of behavior over which he might exercise conscious intention and control. They utilized, in their great experiment, the "new leverage" provided by the emerging self-consciousness. That is, they sought to bring man's genital drives so within the range of his understanding and "objectifying consciousness" that he could learn to connect them with particular ideals and persons.

How did courtly love effect this integration? It did it by opening up the structure of rational consciousness to *degrees* of sexual feeling, allowing only those aspects of sexual behavior to enter into a personal relationship that could be kept under control. It did it by "symbolizing" the sexual act, that is, by linking every sexual act with a personal thought and intention so that whatever was done "meant" more than merely the act itself. The courtly lovers had to *learn* how to behave in these new ways.

The genital drive, in its original state, is not linked with human intentions. Sexual intercourse, and its preliminaries, are—in their original state—merely what they are. Hence they do not express an intentional meaning. To make sex an expression of love requires a learning process. The courtly lovers abstained, therefore, from all those aspects of sexual interaction that they could not bring within the range of personal intention and voluntary control. This is why courtly love allowed all forms of sexual communication excepting orgasm alone.

By abstaining from those aspects of sexual behavior that they could not bring under voluntary control, the courtly lovers actually transformed sexual behavior itself. They made it into more than it had been originally. For by abstaining from orgasm, i.e., final private satisfaction, they lengthened the period of personal-sexual intimacy. They created many new forms of sexual interest and expression. In this way, the sexual process became an extended and complex series of steps over which a voluntary control was exercised—much like the American teenager's petting process.

By creating this series of "steps" of increasing intimacy, the courtly lovers broke the power of instinctual sexuality. This instinctual sexuality, or genital drive, aims—in its original untransformed form—at the quickest route to satisfaction. When a man is acting "instinctually," each step necessarily leads to, or fuses with, the next. The mechanism is automatic. In courtly love, however, the inevitability of this instinctual process was broken. Sexual interaction became a series of symbolic-affective steps— each of which had the value of a word, or expression of love. Each step was an end in itself—not just a means to something else. To touch the woman's breast, for example, would not necessarily carry one along to "something else." This could now be experienced as an act which contained a complete meaning and satisfaction. Nor would even vaginal penetration "carry one along" to orgasm. Rather, the coital union could be enjoyed for what it was in itself—and not merely regarded as a means to orgasm. By breaking up the instinctual sexual process into a series of steps (and even creating new forms of sexual pleasure), the courtly lovers destroyed the spontaneity of instinctual sexuality, but created a new and higher form of personal-sexual life.

Once the process of personal-sexual interaction had been broken into a series of "steps," various forms of sexual behavior could be proportioned out in accordance with different situations and differing degrees of intimacy. For example, though the lady and gentleman of courtly love would reserve orgasm for their relation with their marital partners alone, they would engage in various other forms of personal-sexual behavior with other persons. With some, for example, they would carry on romantic conversation. With others, they might share a kiss. And with still others—probably only their dearest love—they might lie naked together, caressing each other and even engaging in coital union without orgasm (*coitus reservatus*).

For persons who have not learned the psychological technique of separating these various forms of sexual behavior from one another—and the practice of proportioning them out with regard to persons, time and places—the practice of courtly love seems simply unbelievable. It is not uncommon to dismiss courtly love as a theory concocted merely to cover up the fact that "just plain sex" was going on. This judgment tells more about the experience of the one who makes it than about courtly love itself. Though there were failures to attain to the ideal, it is now generally conceded by historians of this movement that, however strange this behavior may seem, it was widespread among the late medieval aristocracy. Moreover, that such graded sexual behavior is possible is evidenced by the American adolescent petting process. In this petting process, sexual feelings and drives are gradually personalized and incorporated into the personal love relation by drawing a series of "lines" that allow persons to learn personal-sexual intimacy with each other. An example of such line drawing has been given by the late Albert Kinsey. Analyzing a group of twenty- to forty-year-old women who had at least kissed men but had not had sexual intercourse, Kinsey found the following range of experience. [10]

```
100% = kissing
 74% = deep kissing
 72% = breast manipulation
 32% = oral stimulation of the breast
 36% = received masturbation
 24% = performed masturbation
 17% = contacted bare male genitals with own
  3% = received oral-genital contact
  2% = performed oral-genital contact
```

Recall now, that this is the tabulation of the sexual experience of American female *virgins*. It shows that the American practice of sexual learning (petting) like the practice of courtly love puts a high valuation on two things: (1) physical heterosexual intimacy and (2) the avoidance of coital orgasm. The tension between the two creates a lengthy process of personal-sexual interaction that is "filled" with a series of sexual acts that express ever greater intimacy. These steps are not simply the normal steps one would go through if one were simply engaging in genital behavior in order to attain, in the quickest and most direct way, the goal of orgasm. Rather, these steps are created by the imaginations of the persons involved—and their effect is not simply to heighten the feeling of personal-sexual intimacy, but also to make the sexual process into a series of symbolic acts through which people "talk" with and draw closer to one another.

Romantic conversation, the caressing of the body, the admiration and kissing of the breasts, the lengthy kissing and exploration of the other's mouth with the tongue, the lying together without vaginal penetration, the extension of the period of coital union by reserving orgasm—these are not, as Freud and many others have pointed out, the "natural" and quickest way to attain the goal sought by the autonomous genital drive. They are, in Freud's judgment, "detours," almost *perversions*—for these are self-conscious ways of avoiding orgasm. That they have the effect of heightening psychosexual intimacy, personalizing the sexual interaction, and eroticizing the entire body actually, in Freud's view, counts *against* their naturalness. The "natural" way of ordering the sexual drive— according to Freud and others—is to leave it in its segmented autonomous condition. But in courtly love, as in the American petting process, there is a break with this primitive patriarchal conception of sex. After courtly love, the ideal goal of sexual encounter is not private orgasm, but a heightened experience by two persons of communion and intimacy with each other. After courtly love, the purpose of sex can be neither orgasm, nor procreation, nor pleasure, but personal communication and communion. The emergence of this new use of sex for communication awaited the evolution of self-consciousness in man.

[European commentators on "petting"—which is a uniquely American method of sexual learning that continues the tradition of courtly love—are almost unanimous in their judgment that it is a sexual perversion or *"Umweg."* They, like Freud, are victims of the pre-modern experience of sex that assumes the genital drive should remain an autonomous instinctual mechanism. It is obvious that only those persons who learn to personalize the sexual drive (through some such learning process as petting) can ever experience that drive as anything other than an autonomous instinctual mechanism that seeks the quickest and most direct way to orgasm. The different American judgment about the possibility of personalizing and voluntarizing the genital drive expresses, actually, the new experience of the sexual drive that is learned through the petting process.]

We shall now consider how the second possiblity for human sexual behavior implied by self-consciousness was also learned: the new psychosexual *intimacy* between men and women. The development of self-consciousness, we noted earlier, opens up a kind of duality within the self. In *self*-consciousness, a man experiences himself as both himself and the one experiencing himself. He realizes what it is to be both himself and "another," both another and "himself." He experiences an inner interpersonal richness at the center of his own consciousness.

It is a difficult thing to explain this experience to those who have not had it—and it is still a rare thing to find in its heightened form. But, for example, the development of self-consciousness allows a man to orient himself in terms of himself. He can orient himself in terms of a conscious *self*-awareness. He no longer needs to maintain the constancy of his beliefs and the consistency of his actions by orienting himself on things outside himself. Rather, he can live by carrying on an inner conversation, an inner dialogue, and an inner self-orientation. It is precisely this fact that opens up for modern men a wholly new experience, an experience of a kind no previous man ever had before—namely, *psychological* experience or the self's conscious experience of itself. Those who have read in the history of literature know how seldom before modern times persons recorded their own feelings about themselves and their inner lives. This is not simply because they were disinterested in recording such psychological experiences. It is, rather, because such experiences were unavailable to men before the emergence of *self*-consciousness.

When, now, we think about the *modern* conception of love between a man and a woman, we immediately see how much it not only presupposes but also gives expression to this new kind of psychological experience. The topic of greatest interest in the romantic novels—beginning in the late seventeenth and eighteenth centuries—is precisely the inner feeling and orientation of the person in love. The person in love begins to be self-conscious of his feelings and to report how he feels. Love begins to be experienced as a unique and heightened form of self-consciousness. To tell a person you love her means to tell her how you feel, how you are aware of yourself, in her presence. It is to tell her how being intimately related to her makes you aware of a new relation of yourself to yourself. In modern times, love becomes—for the first time in human history—the experience of psychological intimacy. This psychological intimacy cannot exist without self-consciousness—and it is created by *conversation.*

The "petting process" is the technique by which men learn to gain voluntary control over their sexual behavior, and personal conversation is the method by which the new experience of intimate psychological love is created. Through personal conversation, by which persons expose their innermost feelings to each other and thereby share in each other's psychological lives, persons are spiritually united. Through conversation, they are bound together in a psychological union that is much deeper and closer than the coital union of their bodies. For when persons tell each other how they experience themselves when they are present to each other, each one begins to experience the other as that other experiences himself.

For example, to the degree that I can tell another how I feel when I am close to her, to that same degree she can know me as I know myself. To the degree that I am self-conscious about my feelings (that is, to the degree that I can objectify them and express them in speech), to that same degree she can share them with me. Without self-consciousness and the intimate conversation that springs from it, there can be no psychological and spiritual communion. And precisely to the degree that such intimate and open conversation is possible, two persons can become one in soul.

Within the tradition of courtly love, the essence of love was understood to be this spiritual conversation. That is, the essence of love was understood to be the act of joining two souls in an intimate union of mutual understanding and affection that was created by the power of speech alone. This is why, within courtly love, kissing the mouth was regarded as a preeminent act of physical affection. For genital union is a way of uniting only bodies, but kissing is a way of uniting oneself with that part of the body that is the organ of the soul. Through the mouth, not through the genitals, the true intercourse between a man and woman is created. Hence the act of kissing is the act of honoring and loving the organ through which spiritual communion is sustained.

I recall once taking a philosophy seminar where the question at stake was whether one should carry on conversation while engaged in sexual intercourse. At the time I recall being unimpressed by the importance of the question, but startled by the professor's insistence that without such conversation the act of intercourse is intrinsically deficient. It took some aging for me to appreciate the issue. Perhaps, to illustrate it, we might recall the scene between Benjamin and Mrs. Robinson in *The Graduate*. After their torrid sexual relationship has run through its earliest stages, Benjamin decides it is not fully satisfying just to go to bed with Mrs. Robinson. He wants to personalize his relation to her. He wants to have a conversation. In a marvellously ironic way, the movie brings out the contrast between the two ideals of sexual relationship— the communitive and the orgasmic ideals. A recent movie criticism takes Benjamin to task for failing to appreciate Mrs. Robinson's "healthy instinctual sexuality." But the problem is that Mrs. Robinson is totally incapable of a personal relation with anyone—and hence is incapable of knowing anything about *genital love*. Benjamin, on the other hand, finds the body of Mrs. Robinson uninteresting after he realizes that a purely genital relation with her cannot be a way of establishing a personal union. His is the ideal of courtly love—which now serves also as the American sexual ideal.

The stress upon personal intimacy and conversation as essential ingredients of love has a transformative effect upon male and female identity in modern societies. In pre-modern societies, it is not only impossible for psychologically intimate conversation to exist between men and women, but it is also the case that men and women tend not to be friends with or to converse with each other. In pre-modern societies, all conversation, hence personal friendship, is normally among persons of the same sex. This, in part, explains the separation of sex and love in earlier times. But the lack of personal conversation between men and women has yet another effect; it leads to men and women defining themselves as contraries, as beings who are essentially unable to understand each other.

When, in modern times, men and women begin to converse with each other, their definitions of male and female identity begin to change. In intimate conversation, when a man tells a woman how he feels and vice versa, there is the possibility for a woman to take into herself, by an act of empathetic imagination, the self-feeling of the man. She can, if she then wishes, identify with a person of a different sex. And the man can also, in this way, learn to identify with the feelings of a woman. Through psychologically revelatory conversation, therefore, men become more feminine and women become more masculine. Each begins to identify with something in the other—as each seeks to please and enjoy the other. Through this intimacy, a tendency toward *psychological bisexuality* is generated. Women become "masculinely feminine" and men become "femininely masculine." For example, here is Morton Hunt's description of this tendency toward psychological bisexuality as it took place in courtly love. There was, Hunt notes, a major change in manners produced by courtly love on the noblemen of the late middle ages.

These fierce semi-primitive chieftains had begun to cultivate the arts of singing, dancing, and composing in order to please the ladies of their courts. They put on finer clothing, started to use handkerchiefs, and began to bathe more often; they practiced gentle discourse and sophisticated argumentation . . . and squandered both money and health on endless jousts and harrowing pilgrimages designed to gain merit in their ladies' eyes.[11]

The noblemen of courtly love became more feminine. But it is no less important to note that the noblewomen of courtly love also became more masculine. They came to enjoy the jousts and hunts and duels of the men and to take part in them themselves—exactly as the young American coed develops an interest in basketball or football because of her close friendship with men who are interested in these sports. Hence, in courtly love as in America, the ideal of personal intimacy as the determining feature of personal-sexual love leads toward psychological bisexuality, toward the man's beginning to value for himself what the woman feels and the woman's beginning to enjoy what the man values. In this way, heightened self-consciousness tends to break down sexual identification and interaction in terms of complementary male-female roles.

Let us turn now to a third aspect of courtly love: the development and significance of stylized manners in which men show special respect for women. In America today, such politeness—or stylized ways of allowing women to have precedence over men—are taken for granted. The man holds the woman's coat for her, opens the door for her, rises when she enters the room, carries her parcels, and treats her with deference. To-day, when such politeness is under attack by the woman's liberation movement, it may be of interest to recall the origins of such behavior and the purpose it originally served.

In the Western world, because of the triumph of Hebrew patriarchalism, the woman was relegated to a position of inferiority vis-à-vis the man. She was, as we have already seen, subordinated to man in both her social and her sexual life. In Hebrew patriarchy, the relative equality—or complementarity—of men and woman characteristic of tribal societies was destroyed.

When, in courtly love, there was an effort to create personal equality and intimacy between men and women—at least in the courtly love relationship—there had to be some way to overcome the social and sexual inequality of woman that still persisted from the older patriarchal tradition. The social and sexual inequality had to be overcome in order that the lovers could be truly friends and truly open to each other. (Friendship and personal love presuppose the equality of the partners.) Courtly love presumed the notion that men and women are spiritually equal, but it had to create a means to make them socially and sexually equal. It had to find some way to compensate for the social and sexual subordination of women to men that stemmed from the patriarchal tradition.

The function of courtly love manners was to compensate for the traditional inferior position of women vis-à-vis men. Since, in ordinary late medieval society, women were still assumed to be socially inferior, social equality between a man and a woman could be established only by showing women—in a stylized way—special preference. Courtly love manners are not, of course, ways of treating women as full and perfect equals. Rather, courtly love manners are ways of compensating for the inferiority of women in order to establish an equality between the partners.

By compensating for the social inferiority of women, courtly love raised the status of women until, today, the actual effect of such courtly practices is precisely the opposite of what it was originally. This is because once women and men are social equals, the continued use of stylized symbols of deference toward women serves to generate *inequality* between men and women. The effect of courtly manners today is, therefore, precisely the opposite of what it was originally. This is why the woman liberationists protest against "being treated like ladies." It is because "being treated like ladies" today suggests an inequality between men and women, implies that women are really inferior to men and not able to do things for themselves. The very manners that, at first, created social equality between men and women now stand against its full realization. This is, of course, because such manners were originally *compensating practices.*

The compensating character of courtly manners needs to be understood in the context of medieval feudal society. In medieval society, each person occupied a fixed social rank. Each person showed a stylized deference to those persons above him, and those above acknowledged this deference by protecting those below. Hence, a medieval serf showed respect for his lord; the lord showed respect for his duke; the duke showed respect toward his king. Within this system, it was a mark of respect for knights to rise when their lord appeared, for knights to assist their lords with their cloaks, for knights to wait on their lords and show them general deference. Such practices are not wholly out of style even today. It is, for example, normal for an employee to rise when his higher-up bosses enter his office. Such deferential practices are ways of acknowledging sovereignty and of showing honor.

The essence of courtly love manners is nothing other than men's beginning to show that same stylized deference toward women that they showed for their superiors in the feudal system. Just as the knight would rise for his king, so he now begins to rise for his lady. Just as the knight assisted the king with his cloak, so he now begins to assist his lady. In this way, he treats her as if she occupied a higher social position than he. (The knight would not, of course, rise for his wife—for not the wife, but the lady, is the object of courtly love.) Through such deferential practices, the socially subordinate position of women in medieval society was compensated for and a social equality was created.

Of course, not all such courtly practices were merely compensatory "social fictions." It was usually the case that the lady actually occupied a higher social position than her courtly lover. Preferably a knight would court not the wife of his social equal, but the wife of his social superior. For example, Sir Lancelot paid court to Queen Guinevere. By paying court "up" the social ladder, the courtly lover reversed the pattern of patriarchal marriage—where the man marries "down."

Another aspect of this compensatory process was the fact that the courtly lover frequently paid court to a woman who was not only higher in social position, but also relatively older than he. This, too, reversed the usual pattern of patriarchal marriage—where older men marry younger women and, by virtue of their greater experience, are able to dominate them. But a personal relation between a man and a relatively older woman allowed her to bring to the relationship a range of maturity, self-confidence, and experience that further heightened possibilities for equality and intimacy between herself and her lover. Not all these possibilities were realized, of course, in the early centuries of courtly love. But, over the centuries, the equalitarian ideal became increasingly important until today—where romantic marriage is valued—it is assumed that a man and his wife will be of relatively equal age.

The various transformations of human behavior discussed above—the creation of elaborate courtly "petting practices," the emergence of the new ideal of love as psychological intimacy, and the development of courtly "manners"—could only take place within a wholly transformed metaphysics, or world view. Just as an individual person's sexual self-image is an evidence for the mode of consciousness in him, so the sexual practices of a total society are manifestations of a total religio-political outlook. The development of courtly love, therefore, not only evidences the emergence of self-consciousness in man, but also evidences the rise of a new form of religion, or theology, in late medieval society.

In the first chapter, we saw how the evolution of ego consciousness gave rise to the patriarchal family and *also* to the patriarchal, monotheistic conception of God as Yahweh (Jehovah). This patriarchal conception of God was later qualified by early Christianity, which conceived God not as an ego (i.e., anthropomorphically), but as a universal rational principle. That is, early Christianity qualified the anthropomorphic Ruler-God of Israel by identifying this God with the metaphysically abstract First Principle of the Greeks. This new metaphysically abstract conception of God was the foundation for the sexual reorientation of the man-woman relation accomplished by Christianity. That is, if God is conceived in metaphysical-rational terms, persons can also be conceived in purely rational terms. Hence, as we have seen, early Christianity and monasticism defined men and women as "rational substances"—and thereby attributed to them equality, but at the price of denigrating their bodies and their sexual differences.

The history of medieval theology is the history of the recovery of the personal conception of God that was first articulated in the Old Testament. But to recover such a personal conception of God meant, for medieval theology, to find a way to combine this notion with the new sense of the male and the female as equal in dignity. This could only be done if medieval theology could develop beyond Old Testament religion and find a way to represent the universal God in *both* male and female persons. This is what Israelite, Old Testament theology had not been able to do. Medieval theology found the way to symbolize divinity in both men and women by elevating Mary to a place of co-dignity (if not precisely co-equality) with Jesus.

A remarkable development of Mariology begins in the eleventh and twelfth centuries—precisely the moment when courtly love was also beginning. The doctrine that Mary was "immaculately conceived" also began to be formulated and celebrated within the Church at this time. "Immaculate conception" means something different from virgin birth. By "immaculate conception" is meant that Mary was conceived in the normal human way, but without sin. In the religion of this time, it was still assumed that all sexual intercourse was sinful because it involved the temporary suspension of man's reason and voluntary freedom by man's passions—at least in the moment of orgasm. To say that Mary was "immaculately conceived" meant, therefore, several things.

First, it meant that Mary—like Jesus—could be regarded as morally sinless. It meant that women could be regarded as fully capable of the highest acts of religious and moral devotion—even when they themselves lived in families and were mothers (i.e., without becoming nuns). The doctrine of the immaculate conception was the Church's way of repudiating its earlier patriarchal depreciations of women, depreciations that are so frequently found in St. Paul, St. Ambrose, and St. Augustine. This doctrine made it possible to think of women as possessing a dignity fully equal to that of man. Hence, if Jesus could be a perfect image of God, so, too, could Mary. A woman, no less than a man, could therefore be an object of spiritual love—which, after all, is what courtly love was all about. In fact, it would not be incorrect to say that courtly love was an analogy to, or social extension of, the religious veneration of Mary. The courtly lover loved his lady as one possessing all perfections, as one who (by the fiction of courtly manners) was higher in dignity than he and a mediator to him of whatever was Good and True. There is, therefore, a relation between the new devotion to Mary that began in the eleventh and twelfth centuries and the beginnings of courtly love.

A second consequence of the doctrine of immaculate conception—a consequence not yet fully explicated by Catholic theology—is that it implies there can be a perfectly sinless act of sexual intercourse. By "perfectly sinless" is here meant an act of sexual intercourse in which there is a perfect congruence of moral intention and sexual feeling. The notion of immaculate conception implies (allowing for the discrepancies between the medieval thought world and our own) that sexual intimacy can be fully moralized and spiritualized—which, of course, is precisely what the courtly lovers were undertaking with their experiments in controlled "petting."

Erich Fromm, and other psychological interpreters of the development of Christian religion, see the medieval development of Mariology as a regression back to the prepatriarchal period of history. They view it as the return of the "Great Mother." But it is not this at all. In fact, precisely what distinguishes medieval Mariology from such a regression is what makes it such a great evolutionary advance. We recall that in prepatriarchal societies, the Mother—as embodiment of the natural process of procreation—is the unity of birth, love, and death. She is both "womb and tomb," both creator and destroyer. She is the one whom to love is to admit one's biological being and finitude, hence to die. (Orgasm is called "the little death.") For example, in F. Fellini's recent movie *The Satyricon,* this "double-faced" Great Mother figure is represented by the witch Oenothea. Oenothea appears to Encolpius, the young hero, as an exquisitely beautiful, enticing woman who—in the moment of his sexual intercourse with her—reveals herself as a bloated, insatiable and devouring harridan. It is this double meaning of the Woman as the symbol of biological nature, the unity of love and death, that makes her such a threat to emerging patriarchal society. For in patriarchal society, men are seeking to find a new form of creative power—one by which men can gain freedom over biological nature so that they can create their own historical destinies.

The Great Mother, therefore, is both a Life Figure and a Death Figure. This is what makes her both bewitching and witchy. What happens in medieval religion, however, is that woman is freed from this "biological" duality—just as, in patriarchal religion, man freed himself from it. Mary is not a symbol of the Great Mother. Rather, Mary is a symbol of Woman as an unambivalent symbol of Love and Life. The negative side, the death side, that was part of the Great Mother symbol has been eliminated from her. Hence, the development of Mariology is not a regression to the *Great Mother* but the evolution of a new and unambivalent symbol of woman. Mary is the symbol of woman now released from her dual symbolization of both Love and Death. Mary is the symbol of Pure Love, of Love that does not seek to snare, possess, and devour. Mary is the symbol of Love that liberates, inspires, creates. Mary represents woman as no longer "the hostage that binds man to fortune," but as man's inspiration to seek his own highest aspirations.

This is not yet precisely what the Women's Liberation Movement truly desires. For women to be man's inspiration is not yet for her to be man's true companion. It is a false kind of "equality" that is here being created. But this medieval moment is, historically, a time of compensation where the radical subordination of woman can be overcome only by overidealizing her.

The problem, however, is that in all these transformations of his religious symbols, man is also reconstructing his own inner psychological life. To demythologize and moralize the symbol of woman by eliminating those aspects which represent human finitude, shortcoming, and death from it does not, in itself, eliminate the negative elements from the psychology of man. *These* still are there—and though they are not projected on Mary or the lady of courtly love, they do find their symbolization and expression. In the late Middle Ages, therefore, alongside the symbol of Mary and the Lady appears a second image of woman—the image of woman who represents only the negative side of the Great Mother. That woman is the Witch.

Historians have frequently commented on the sudden emergence, in the twelfth and thirteenth centuries, of a whole new theory of witchcraft and the systematic persecution of witches. This preoccupation with, and persecution of, witches continues for several centuries, finally coming to an end only with the Enlightenment. For example, Thomas Aquinas, the great theologian of the thirteenth century, introduces a lengthy section on witches into Catholic theology. Martin Luther, the Protestant Reformer, believed he actually experienced a personal devil—as did St. Ignatius, the sixteenth century founder of the Jesuits. In Salem, Massachusetts, toward the end of the seventeenth century, several persons were condemned to death for witchcraft.

It is noteworthy that the period of persecution of witches is exactly identical with the period of courtly love. How can we explain this peculiar fact? The Witch, I suggest, was nothing other than the counterface of the Lady. She was the one who objectified all those anxieties and negative feelings that late medieval man could not allow to enter into his imagination and feelings about his Lady. Since the Lady had to be all good, there had to be someone to carry the unconscious fears man had that she *might not* really be all good—but also somewhat threatening. That is the function of the witch. She is the counterface of the Lady; she is the one on whom medieval man projected his fears of woman.

The history of witchcraft is, of course, much longer than merely the period of the late Middle Ages. But in this longer history, the figure of the witch is much more diffuse and much less bound up with sexuality. In the late medieval period under discussion, witchcraft takes on three new characteristics. (1) Witches become a major problem for theology and philosophy. (2) Witches are systematically persecuted and executed by government and ecclesiastical bodies. (3) Witches are specifically identified as having their power through being sexually united with the Devil and through inflicting upon men various sexual afflictions. The witch, during the period of courtly love, is associated with the transformation of sexual identity and behavior.

We can understand why medieval witchcraft developed in conjunction with courtly love when we think about the anxiety men faced as they, for the first time in Western history, tried to approach women openly as sexual friends and equals. Everything in man's past had been such as to make him experience sexual encounter as aggressive, as a relation where one person manifested power over the other. We have seen, for example, how much the exaggerated authority of the male over the female in the patriarchal system also was a defense against unconscious anxieties about the sexual power of woman. For men to begin to behave toward women in a new way, approaching them not with aggression, but with openness and intimate caring, was a brave thing. No matter how much man tried to believe there was no danger in this open kind of love, the older fear about the power of woman still was at work in him. It is this older fear that was first objectified and then catharsized in the figure of the Witch.

CHAPTER VI

The Romantic Revolution

THE American Puritans, and spiritualists such as the Quakers, developed the romantic principle of courtly love to its ultimate form. They did what courtly lovers had never dared to do; by combining the romantic love relation and the marriage relation, they created the new social institution of *romantic marriage.*

Within courtly love, it had always been understood that romantic lovers would never be husband and wife. In fact, it was a maxim that if courtly lovers were to marry each other then each was under an obligation to seek another romantic love relation. Whatever the achievements of courtly love, it still presumed the age-old separation of procreative sex and personal love.

Romantic marriage is a revolutionary institution because it radically transforms both the relation between the husband and the wife and their relation to their own children. In this way, romantic marriage forces a total restructuring of society. First, it destroys the age-old patriarchal subordination of the female to the male. The essence of romantic love is the equality of the partners. Second, it displaces the parent-child relation from a primary to a secondary position within the family. That is, romantic marriage makes the primary purpose of marriage the love of the husband and the wife for each other, subordinating their intention to have children or to gain economic security to this end. Romantic lovers marry so that they may be, first and foremost, husband and wife —not so that they may be, first and foremost, father and mother. The primary purpose of their marriage is to facilitate their enjoying an ever-growing intimacy with each other, and this and this alone is sufficient reason for them to marry. In romantic marriage, the husband and the wife do not need children to hold their own relation together. The woman is not constantly defining herself in terms of the role of "mother." In romantic marriage, therefore, parents do not need to hold on to their children, but can allow them to leave home and establish lives of their own. Romantic marriage both presupposes and encourages the development of *individuality.*

In America, this acceptance of the fundamental value of romantic love implies a correspondingly high valuation of individuality. For romantic love is that inner feeling, or sense of heart, that is able to discern the uniqueness of persons. It is that feeling which is able to recognize the sense in which one woman is different from every other woman in the world—and one man is unlike every other man. Because it discerns the uniqueness of persons, romantic love as the foundation of marriage encourages the development of an individualistic society.

[Ralph Waldo Emerson extols the way in which romantic love leads to an experience of the uniqueness of persons. The man who loves in this way, notes Emerson, "does not longer appertain to his family and society. *He* is a person. *He* is a soul."

Romantic love discerns the uniqueness of persons, and the ability to love and be loved in this way makes a person unique. It bestows upon him an identity that transcends all social and familial roles. For this reason, continues Emerson, "the lover never sees personal resemblances in his mistress to her kindred or others. His friends find in her a likeness to her mother, or her sisters, or to persons not of her blood. The lover sees no resemblance except to summer evenings and diamond mornings, to rainbows and the song of birds."[12]

What happens in a society that accepts this kind of love as the foundation for marriage and the family? There will be a strong impetus in the direction of individualism within all social structures. But it also means that the essential purpose of marriage will be to allow two persons to share their own unique relation—rather than to fulfill some natural or social function.]

The rise of romantic marriage and its validation by the Puritans and spiritualists (such as Emerson) represents a major innovation within the Christian tradition. A whole new notion of man and the meaning of marriage emerges for the first time. In early Christianity, procreation was still assumed to be the primary purpose of marriage. This early Christian view has been reiterated by the Catholic Church at the Second Vatican Council. In describing marriage, the Council argued that

Marriage and conjugal love are by their nature ordained toward begetting and educating of children. Children are really the supreme gift of marriage and contribute very substantially to the welfare of their parents. The God Himself who said "It is not good for man to be alone" (Genesis 2:18) and "who made man from the beginning male and female" (Mark 19:4) wished to share with man a certain participation in His own creative work. Thus He blessed male and female, saying: "Increase and multiply" (Genesis 1:28).[13]

Notice that this argument reinterprets the phrase "It is not good for man to be alone," which in Genesis refers to the male's being without a female, to mean that it is not good for a husband and wife to be without children. According to Vatican II, for a man and a woman to be fully and properly husband and wife, they must first be father and mother. The former roles are regarded as dependent upon the latter (i.e., in "order of nature," not in "order of time"). However, following the second axial transition, there was a reversal of this order, a reversal that became decisive for spiritualistic-individualistic Protestantism. (This modern form of Protestantism, stemming from the Puritans and the Quakers, is essentially different from the Anglicanism, Lutheranism, and Calvinism of the sixteenth-century Reformation.)

In spiritualistic-individualistic Protestantism, the primary purpose of marriage is understood to be the sexual communion and personal affection of the husband and wife for each other. Procreation becomes, on this view, a nonessential good. That is, children are not regarded as *complet-*

ing the couple or *fulfilling* the marriage. They may be desired and valued, but for their own sake. They are an "extra benefit" *(bene esse)*. A couple, however, may legitimately prefer to do without such extras. The integrity of the marriage itself requires only the personal love of the husband and wife.

This spiritualistic Protestant outlook has become the American ideal. In the American perspective, the roles of father/mother derive from the roles husband/wife. This means that in America marriage is given priority over the family—a reversal of the traditional order seen in the above statement from Vatican II. This is why men and women today marry for love of each other rather than to fulfill any obligation to beget children or to continue the ethnic family line. And this is why, in modern culture, a new basis for divorce has emerged: mutual incompatibility. This development actually strengthens modern marriage, for it makes clear that marriage depends upon the continuing consent and love of the married pair for each other.

Romantic marriage is absolutely personalistic. The purpose of the relationship is defined wholly in terms of the desires and agreements of the two persons involved. Romantic marriage is essentially a private contract. Unlike traditional marriage, romantic marriage has no "natural" social or biological function to which the partners must conform if they are to be truly married. (Vatican II says, opposing this romantic notion of marriage, that "Marriage and conjugal love are *by their nature* ordained to the begetting and educating of children.")

In premodern societies, marriage is never understood personalistically because the experience of full human individuality has not yet evolved. Rather, in traditional societies, marriage is understood to be a social institution that has a permanent and impersonal natural function to which the partners must conform if they are to be truly married. The partners cannot agree what their marriage is to be; they become married by adapting themselves to some larger social and biological purpose. In the West, the argument about the essential purpose of marriage has focused on the act of procreation. In the East, however, it is assumed that a no less essential purpose of marriage is to provide care for the parents and grandparents in their old age.

In India, a "natural" purpose of marriage is to provide security and religious burial for the elders. Because this is understood to be an essential purpose of marriage, it is quite understandable that parents would arrange the marriages of their children. They do so because the purpose of marriage is defined in terms of the interests of the parent generation rather than in terms of the two people getting married. We can understand why, in this situation, the question whether the bride and groom personally love each other is relatively unimportant. Because the parent-child relation is more important than the husband-wife relation in traditional societies, it is also quite understandable that the natural purpose of sexual relations will be understood to be procreation rather than the expression of personal love and affection. (Such social considerations explain why the mere distribution of contraceptives in India is not sufficient to make people understand why they should want to use contraceptives. If you cannot really understand any other reason for sex than procreation, then why in the world would you want contraceptives?)

In the West, Catholicism, Judaism, and Lutheranism still regard the procreation of children as an essential purpose of marriage. Within these traditions, it is still assumed that a couple may not agree between themselves not to have any children at all (except in the most extenuating circumstances).

Romantic marriage is a new institution created as part of the major social revolution that began in the Western world in the seventeenth century. This revolution created, in addition to romantic marriage, the democratic state and the free contract capitalistic economy. In this revolution, a major reversal of the traditional relation between persons and social institutions was effected. Whereas before the seventeenth century men assumed that social institutions are stable and should be defined in terms of enduring essences or functions that should never be altered by individuals, after the seventeenth century men began to assume that social institutions should be reconstructed to meet the wishes of individuals. Before the seventeenth century, men assumed that they should adapt to society. After the seventeenth century, men began to reconstitute society and make it adapt to individual men.

This seventeenth-century development presupposes an evolution in human consciousness, an evolution that extends to society the discoveries of the late medieval period of history. Just as the courtly lovers created a "psychological technology" to reconstruct their instinctual feelings and to create new kinds of relations between men and women, so the Puritans and spiritualists began to develop "social technologies" to reorganize the societies in which they lived. This seventeenth-century development is significant, but it is not really a major "axial" transition. It is, rather, a further development of self-consciousness—an extension of self-consciousness into the social world in which man lives.

For human beings even to imagine the possibility of romantic marriage implies that they are, in terms of their mode of consciousness, different from all other human beings who have ever lived. The mode of consciousness that undergirds the idea of romantic marriage is different from the mode of consciousness, or self-image, that was implied by courtly love. Courtly love presupposed the emergence of individual self-consciousness. It presupposed that men had begun to have a sense of themselves as unique beings and could also regard other persons in this same way. But the mere experience of self-consciousness and the uniqueness of persons was, at first, something experienced "inside" man alone. Hence, the courtly lovers did not attempt to change traditional social institutions. They accepted the traditional form of marriage and the family and created a new kind of love that coexisted alongside these. Hence, courtly love did not attempt a total social revolution.

By the seventeenth century, however, man's self-consciousness bursts beyond the purely inner realm of private experience. Men begin to ask whether—given the *uniqueness* of individual persons—the social relations in which they live should not be equally unique. Why should unique persons always have to be related to each other in traditional ways? Why may they not create arrangements that express their own individualities?

In the seventeenth century, men begin to see that social institutions are not timeless and unchangeable, but have developed over the course of history. Once men become socially conscious in this way, they are able to argue that institutions have no "essential nature" or "natural purpose" that must be preserved and to which men must adapt. They are able to see that what has been traditionally regarded as "natural" is merely the expression of an ancient convention. They begin to understand that the world men see about them is but the expression of their own inner needs and desires. For these reasons, men begin, in the seventeenth century, to reconstruct their societies and the natural world about them.

This effort at social reconstruction soon begins to have a feedback effect on men's psychological experience. Men begin to see that if social institutions are reconstructed, children will grow up learning to feel and think of themselves in completely new ways. To create new social institutions, to allow men to have new kinds of social experience, is to create new kinds of men. The social experience is internalized in persons who live through it. It forms in them new psychological orientations.

To reconstruct a society—to create a genuine revolution—one must not simply change the outer arrangements, but must create totally new psychological orientations in the members of a society. Since these psychological orientations are formed in infants and young people, no institution is more crucial for the life of a society than marriage and the family. The creation of a new form of marriage is revolutionary, and it is what distinguishes American society from every other society in the world. We have already seen that romantic marriage reinforces the sense that every person is unique. We shall, in this chapter, consider three other revolutionary consequences of romantic marriage—how it transforms our sense of time, our attitudes toward authority, and our experience of space.

We have seen that in traditional societies one of the important functions of marriage is to provide security for the grandparent generation. The larger, social effect of this definition of marriage is to make not simply the family, but indeed the whole society, *past-oriented*. The family exists for the sake of preserving and caring for what has gone before. In China, for example, the family was an institution that served to keep alive the power and interests of the ancestors and to make the present serve the past.

Romantic marriage breaks with this pattern and frees a married couple, and eventually a whole society, to live for the present and the future. When two persons can make their own marital choices, can please themselves and disregard the wishes of their parents, a whole new time orientation is created within a society. Hence, social change is not simply consistent with personal, or romantic, marriage. It is actually created by it. Is it merely an accident that of all the peoples of Europe, the men who had the courage first to leave their homelands and settle in America were predominantly Puritans and spiritualists—those in whom the ideal of personal marriage had come to fullest consciousness?

Moreover, once this new attitude toward time is learned, so that people begin to live in terms of the future and in terms of social change, personal marriage helps to maintain the kind of identity needed by highly mobile persons. Personal marriage allows every person to share a continuous experience with at least one intimate friend throughout all the geographical and vocational relocations and removals that a rapidly changing society requires. Without the possibility of sharing and conversing about one's history with another, it would be difficult for a person to bind all the novelties of his life into a continuous story and thereby construct a "symbolic" identity. Personal identity in changing societies is always symbolic: it is constructed through the artifices of memory and symbol, through the device of autobiography. But the enlivening and support of such memory is strengthened by the presence of another. Personal marriage provides us with a friend who shares, confirms, and expands historical memory, thereby sustaining that symbolic identity which a changing society presupposes. The husband and the wife alone are permanently committed to travel the same road and to share the future as they have shared the past. Only friends and lovers could do this with and for each other, for what they most love is the other himself.

[There has not yet been sufficient attention to those psychological and social developments that were prerequisite to large-scale family immigration, such as was characteristic of early America. But, for example, Erik Erikson offers the following reflection: "First, a word, then, on the decision to migrate. Daniel Lerner recently asked Turkish villagers where, if they had to emigrate, they would go. Many were too horrified even to think of alternatives: it would seem 'worse than death,' they said. The early American immigrants, however, did make that one desperate decision to pick themselves up, as it were, by their roots, a decision which eventually forced them to create a new 'way of life,' that is, new sources and patterns of personal and industrial energy and a new ideological orientation. They chose change, to actively transplant old roots, and then were forced to find new roots in Change itself.""[4]]

Romantic, or personal, marriage is revolutionary in yet another respect. It is the cradle of democratic feeling, the seedbed of opposition to traditional authority. In the traditional patriarchal family, the relation of the wife to the husband is defined as one of obedience to his authority. In such a family, the parent-child relation is also authoritarian—a consistent extension of the husband-wife relation. Just as, in a patriarchal family, the wife is subordinate to her husband, so, in a patriarchal family, the children are subordinate to their parents. Every relationship within the patriarchal family is hierarchical. This means that whenever two people are related, it is always presumed that one is "higher" and the other is "lower." One leads, the other follows. Traditionally, age has preference over youth; maleness over femaleness. The wife obeys the husband, the children obey the mother, the sisters obey the brothers. What is crucial in this pattern is that nothing ever teaches one how to deal with an equal. This explains why the structure of the patriarchal family impedes the development of personal freedom, equality, and friendship.

The patriarchal family is the enemy of democracy because it inculcates a psychological orientation that is incapable of dealing with equalitarian, voluntary relationships. Contemporary sociological research shows that the patriarchal family makes children permanently susceptible to, even eager for, being guided by authority. It makes them *Autoritätsfähig*, that is, capable of functioning well only in hierarchical relations. Once an individual has learned such "authority-readiness," then he needs to be under authority—or to be wielding authority—in order to maintain his identity and sense of well-being.

The *Autoritätsfähig* individual does not experience a democratic equalitarian situation as an opportunity for exercising free initiative. He does not like people to approach him in an equalitarian way. Such experiences are psychologically disorienting for him. He experiences them as threats. Hence, he rejects democratic leadership, preferring even brutally authoritarian forms of government to those forms that allow him personal freedom. He feels safe only when he is unfree.

Contemporary European political thinkers have related the prevalence of totalitarian government in certain countries to the prevalence of the patriarchal family. For it is in such patriarchal families that an authority-readiness is learned, that children become psychologically prepared for an authoritarian state. For this reason, many European thinkers are currently arguing that a genuine social revolution must begin with a revolution in the family.

Dietrich Haensch, for example, argues that the traditional patriarchal, moral condemnation of all sexual relations outside of marriage tends to drive people into marriage. For if people have sexual desires and feel these can be legitimately expressed only within marriage and then only in conjunction with the procreation of children, they are psychologically "eager" for marriage. In this way, patriarchal sexual morality inculcates a "marriage eagerness" for the patriarchal father-mother-child family. Haensch continues:

Second: The traditional triadic structure of the family (father-mother-child) prepares the child for the authority structures of society at large. In the family, the child learns to adapt to authoritarian hierarchies. That is, he internalizes the "fact" that some men rule over other men, that there are some "higher-ups" and some "lower-downs," and that some command while others obey.

Third: Woman's situation in traditional marriage and the family—especially with respect to the distribution of work—is determined by her dependence on her husband. Her economic situation is such that, even if her sexual life were not limited to her relation to her husband, she still would have to accept the task of housekeeper.

Fourth: The traditional ideology of "Motherhood" and the "Big Happy Family" are really perversions of the desire of women to have children—since this ideology actually serves only to reinforce the idea that a woman must be married in order to be fulfilled. This ideology manifests itself most clearly with the prohibition of abortion and the discouragement of contraception—especially in relation to unmarried women. [That is, it encourages women to believe that they should be married in order to enjoy a sexual life and, even, children.]

Fifth: The domination of man over woman in the traditional marriage finally results in the control of the man by the woman. Through his patriarchal role in the family, the man is economically, socially, and politically conditioned to accommodate himself to the reigning political and economic world and must accept existing authority structures—and their requirement that he behave himself and be productive in his job.[15]

Through this criticism, Haensch hopes to show how the patriarchal family produces *Autoritätsfähig* individuals who are eager to live within authoritarian political systems. He believes that the patriarchal family actually is the enemy of democracy—since it inculcates the feeling that hierarchical relations among men are most "natural." This is the other side of the claim that romantic marriage and the democratic family actually produce people who are *Freiheitsfähig*, that is, eager for and capable of using freedom.

[It is important for us to realize that many American marriages that began as romantic unions and continue to present themselves to the outer world as personal-equalitarian relationships have actually ceased to be so. The crisis for every romantic marriage comes with the birth of the first child. At this time, the wife can give up the psychologically more demanding role of being a person in her own right and a friend and companion of her husband and fall back upon the psychologically simpler role of being a "mother." It is simpler because she can dominate the child and use the child as a way of dominating her husband. (Notice how often a woman gives as the "reason" for her behavior the fact that she "has to" because of her children!) In America, this regression is given social sanction by the myth of Motherhood, the "Feminine Mystique." Such a myth and mystique is exploited by much of American industry to sell vast quantities of manufactured goods. The more the good "Mother" buys, the more she traps her husband into being a good and obedient worker. And in this way, the psychological failure of their marriage relation is finally revealed.]

It is crucial to realize that by "patriarchal family" is meant a certain *social structure* and not the particular ways in which people behave within that structure. For example, within a patriarchal family, the parents may be very permissive vis-à-vis their children. But this, in itself, does not make their relationship equalitarian. In fact, Dr. Spock, who has been a vigorous advocate of permissive child rearing, also holds a patriarchal view of women, regarding them as having their "natural" fulfillment as wife and mother. Dr. Spock's patriarchal view of women is perfectly consistent with his permissive view of child rearing. For the essence of the patriarchal family is not whether the discipline is permissive or strict, but the actual structure of relationships within the family itself.

Max Horkheimer, a sociologist of the Frankfurt School, has cogently argued that whether parents are firm disciplinarians or highly permissive makes little difference because "The character of the child is developed more as a function of the structure of the family itself than from the conscious intentions and methods used by the parents in training him."[16] For a parent to deal with his child permissively or strictly is still for the *parent* to deal with the child. (In the same way, many husbands rule their wives very permissively—but still rule. For example, one woman remarked to me that her husband let her do whatever she wanted, asking only that she tell him always what she wanted to do!) When children grow up from infancy knowing nothing except life in a hierarchical familial system, then they cannot even imagine—much less ever actually attempt—democratic, equalitarian, give-and-take. From their infancy on, they have experienced only hierarchical relations where one person leads while the other person follows. In their small world they have only experienced (however subtle) people either commanding obedience or obeying commands.

The only way a child can learn democratic give-and-take and realize that there are forms of human interaction that are not hierarchical is to have parents who are related to each other in a personal, nonhierarchical way. When, as in romantic marriage, the husband and the wife are equals and friends, the child experiences, as the primary example of social interaction in his small world, two adults interacting in a democratic way. He learns that authority-and-obedience is not the only possible way of structuring human relations. He learns that persons can be related on the basis of equality, full openness, through conversation and compromise. He himself begins to relate to others, including his parents, in the same way. In this way, persons who are psychologically capable of democratic social life are formed in the nursery of the democratic family.

The implications of the democratic family extend far beyond the family itself. For if a child learns, in his family, not a capacity for obedience, but a capacity for democratic equalitarian interaction, then he *cannot* adjust to an authoritarian society. He cannot accept leadership that simply justifies its actions because it possesses the symbols of authority and high office. He expects that political and educational leaders will treat him as an equal, will seek to justify their decisions to him and explain their actions. If they do not, then he is *psychologically unable* to accept their leadership. Romantic marriage has produced, therefore, precisely that group of students who today revolt against—because they *cannot* accept—traditional academic, religious, political, and social authority. These are the children of upper-middle- and middle-class parents, that is, of those parents who have generally accepted the ideal of personal-romantic marriage. (It is still the case that lower-middle-class families tend to be patriarchal and hence the children from such families are more eager for authoritarian leadership and less capable of managing democratic give-and-take. But the social tendency is toward the general acceptance of the romantic-democratic pattern.)

Romantic marriage, therefore, and the equalitarian parent-child relation have been revolutionary influences in America. The notion that children and parents should be *friends*—an extension of the notion that the husband and wife should be *friends* (the Puritan innovation!)—produces the kind of people who cannot and will not function within authoritarian social institutions. In the democratic family, the child has his "consciousness raised." He learns to think of himself as possessing a dignity equal to that of his parents—and equal to any other man. He learns, as my son once remarked about his grade-school teachers, that his elders are not trying to be authorities, but "like it when I disagree with them." The democratic family, the natural extension of romantic marriage, inculcates a new kind of human consciousness and self-image. The foundations of democratic government, of democratic schools, and democratic religion are precisely the attitudes and habits that are unconsciously learned in this nursery of the psychological life.

[James Sellers has provided a remarkable statement of the relation between equality and leadership in a democratic society. "What," he asks, "is proper equality? It is certainly not the sort of arrangement by which anyone at all, willy-nilly, may expect to assert himself as a leader. Nor does true equality mean that anyone may, at his own option, ask to be exempt from the burdens of leadership. Proper equality is rather the willingness of the citizen to place himself under the leadership *of his equals;* and it is also the willingness to lead, to function in authority *over one's equals.* The point is that these functions are arranged among equals, who continue to be acknowledged as such, even though the functions are not equal. In this kind of community one does not seek to be a master or to have a master *(Autoritätsfähig!),* but to have one's equal as his master, and to exert mastery only as the equal of other men."[17] The place where such complex psychological competences are first learned is the democratic family.]

We have now considered three of the social functions of romantic marriage within a society: it inculcates a higher sense of personal uniqueness and individuality; it frees men from the past and validates social change; and it lays the foundation for equalitarian, nonauthoritarian relations throughout a society. To conclude this chapter, let us consider a fourth concomitant of romantic marriage: the creation of "total voluntary space."

The romantic American effort to voluntarize and moralize the totality of instinctual behavior revolutionizes the conception of the "space" of men and women in society. Before this romantic vision, it was assumed that the *place* of woman was in the home. Her "space," as the German proverb goes, was *Kirche, Küche, und Kinder* (Church, Kitchen, and Nursery). Because men and women were identified with different spaces, they were—in traditional views of man—always thought to be different kinds of beings. Woman was flesh, man was spirit. She had her fulfillment through her children, man had his fulfillment through his work.

The American voluntarization and personalization of sexual behavior breaks through this traditional notion of space. By rejecting the notion that there is an unmodifiable instinctual behavioral residue, a residue not susceptible to full personalization, American society establishes in principle the full equality of men and women in every aspect of life. If, on the other hand, a culture assumes that some aspect of sexual behavior is not subject to this full personalization (voluntary control), then it is committed to the view that either men or women or both are in bondage to biology. When this view is held, it then becomes necessary to limit—at some point or other—the full participation of women (or men) in the life of society. To deny that some instinct cannot be personalized and moralized is to affirm that there is some aspect of human life that must be controlled by society and external authority—because it cannot be controlled by the persons themselves.

If men are thought to be incapable of controlling sexual lust when alone with a woman, or women thought to be unable to resist a male sexual aggressor, then a society will also think it necessary to protect the man and the woman from their instincts by keeping them apart. It will, for example, think it impossible for men and women to work together without their jeopardizing the whole fabric of society. Or if, on the other hand, a society believes that all women are "instinctually" oriented toward having babies and hence cannot be serious about having a career, it will systematically discriminate against women in the job market, claiming they are not wholehearted workers and really not deserving of serious consideration.

When a society, however, assumes the possibility that all sexual and instinctual behavior can be voluntarized and personalized, then its concomitant assumption will be that men and women are, in principle, able to be related on the basis of equality in all aspects of community life. There is no longer any space or work that is now reserved "For Men Only." Rather, men and women can work together in offices, ride on public transportation together, study together in coeducational schools (living in coeducational dormitories)—and even seek to have sexual fun together, since fun in sex is no less out of "place" for women than it is for men. Thus we see that the romantic, or moralized, notions of sexual behavior that characterize American society give support to, even require, a full participation of women in every social institution on the basis of full equality with men. This is what is meant by the American effort to create a "total voluntary space." It means the blending of the moods traditionally characteristic of the familial and the business worlds. Once this occurs, the *public* behavior of men can now become warm, emotional, open, and nonauthoritarian; women can now enter public space, holding jobs that require initiative and rational competence. It even becomes possible for women to accept responsibility for, and authority over, men and their work without compromising either their womanliness or the masculinity of the men with whom they work. There is no longer a radical difference between the mood of the family and the mood of business and bureaucracy. The equality, warmth, and openness characteristic of the one now modifies the more impersonal, uncaring, obediential structures of the other. Everyone can now be friends, and even the most casual contacts will be assumed to be friendly. Such eroticized public behavior is one of the unique characteristics of the United States. But there has been little reflection on the psychological competences and social transformations that have made such unique behavior possible.

Part Three

THE PLAYMATE

CHAPTER VII

Pet Your Playmate

THE question we turn to now is how the complex psychosocial skills required for romantic marriage and democratic society are actually learned. A young American must, in the course of his or her growing up, recapitulate the history of sexual evolution discussed in the previous chapters. He or she must learn things that mankind has learned over a period of thousands of years. It is not surprising, therefore, that the period of psychosexual learning in America will be considerably longer than in traditional societies. Persons will begin full sexual life, begin to have regular sexual intercourse, relatively later than persons in other societies. And they will be much more self-conscious in their learning of sexual behavior and sexual roles.

Let us turn, first, to a consideration of the function of virginity in American society—for virginity is related to the process of sexual learning. In America, the function of virginity is different from the function of virginity in any of the other social systems we have discussed. As we have seen, in ancient Israel the maintenance of virginity was judged to be primarily a male competence, expressed in the ability *to segment*

voluntary from instinctual behavior. In early Christianity, the maintenance of virginity was assumed to be primarily a female competence,
expressed in the ability *to renounce all instinctual behavor.* In American
society, the maintenance of virginity is a competence required of both
males and females, involving the ability *to integrate both instinctual
feelings and rational volitions in the complex unity of a personal relationship.* Only in this way can sex and love be united; only in this way can
sexual pleasure be incorporated within the new kind of symbolic identity
needed for modern life; only in this way can we have the personal
marriage of erotic friendship that assists identity confirmation in a
changing world.

How is this kind of integrated sexual behavior learned? Although it
might be agreed that there is some kind of aggressive sexual intercourse
that is natural and not learned, it is clear that the sexual competences
required by American society are acquired through a long process of
sexual experimentation and "line-drawing." Dating, including that long
process of increasing sexual intimacy sometimes called "petting," is a
highly stylized institution. By means of a mutual experimentation between adolescent males and females possessing relatively equal degrees
of inexperience, a gradual increase in sexual knowledge, self-knowledge,
and intimate knowledge of others is attained so that the primordial
anxiety associated with sexual intercourse is overcome. Once this occurs,
and the goal of this experimentation is that it should occur, heterosexual
communication can be managed on the basis of continuing mutual consent and without aggression. Moreover, once the personal and technical
competences necessary for maintaining this kind of intimacy are attained, the process of sexual intercourse can be adjusted by constant
feedback so as to yield maximum pleasure for both partners. The American ideal of a "simultaneous orgasm" presupposes just such personal and
technical competences as are learned through this process of adolescent
sexual education. It is important to realize that this process of sexual
education—the pattern of dating and petting that extends over many
years—is uniquely American. Outside America, it is hardly understood,
much less practiced.

Because this process of American sexual education involves the relative equality and inexperience of the partners, it is an "experimental" method of learning. This method of sexual education is an alternative to the typically European method of sexual initiation whereby an older, experienced person introduces a younger, inexperienced one into adult sexual life. The European method of initiation inculcates a greater separation of sexual feeling and personal identity than is consistent with the American ideal of personal-sexual integration. In American sexual education, peer group friends tentatively explore themselves and each other within clearly defined zones of permissible intimacy. The lines that define these zones may be a matter of explicit agreement between the sexual pair, but more often these permissible limits are implicitly decided in the peer group conversation about sex.

To be physically intimate, but to observe strictly the line dividing the permissible from the yet unknown, is the essence of adolescent sexual morality in American society. The issue is not whether one should be sexually intimate, but how far one should go. As each unit of experience is mastered and integrated into the personal relation, enlarging the "social self," another still more intimate sexual unit is opened for exploration. During the years of adolescence the "line" is redrawn again and again in order to allow—rather, to encourage—an ever-increasing experiment in intimacy. By this method, supported by various dating procedures, peer group practices, parental permissiveness, and ritually formalized opportunities for appropriate privacy, the total process of sexual behavior is broken down into a sequence of units that can be serially explored and then integrated within a total personal relationship.

The American petting process, like the practice of courtly love, utilizes the practice of "line-drawing" in order to hold the expression of sexual feeling within the limit susceptible to rational voluntary control. This means that it places a high valuation both on virginity and on physical intimacy. It is precisely the tension between these two values that generates an area of "intimacy" that is open for sexual learning. In this way, boys and girls gradually acquire the complex psychological competences that personal-romantic marriage requires: the full integration of rational and sexual behavior, the willingness to expose intimate feelings to one another, the ability to cope with the exposure of another's anxieties and hostilities, and the courage to resist fleeing from the dynamic equilibrium of total personal intercourse to a less stressful domination or submission. But a person can manage this complex, integrated sexual behavior only if he first learns how to do it: if he first learns of both the intimate parts of his own body and the bodies of those he loves by a tender exploration, if he first learns the reciprocal unveiling of souls from tender conversation, if he first learns to understand himself by understanding another's understanding of him.

In this sexual learning process, a person's social self is formed. A person attains "social self-understanding" when he learns his effect on others and the effect of others on him. In this same way he also gains some practical understanding of the instinctual drives that are hidden in him and in others by expressing them in a trusting context (thereby "objectifying" them) so that they might be felt and seen and talked about. Talked about incessantly! Youth's talking about sex—a conversation that seems to many elders to be profitless, if not depraved—is, in fact, the way in which they come to understand their deepest anxieties and aspirations. They are not talking about sex; they are learning about their true selves. It is the method by which they bring the instinctual into consciousness, the way they integrate their sexual feelings within their personal world.

How important such talking is for helping adolescents learn to understand and gain personal control over their sexual feelings can be appreciated by noting the discomfiture of young adolescents. All sexual situations cause them inner anxiety. The young adolescent boy flees from females, even from his mother.(!) The young adolescent girl is giggly and alternately teasing and frightened. Boys and girls are unsure of themselves precisely because they are dimly aware of changes going on inside of them. After all, it is *they* who are changing and not their external world. How can they gain control over this situation?

In America, control is gained by talking with one another. Let me offer an experience from my own family. When the first of our children's friends began "kissing the girls in the grass" (that's a direct report!), it created great excitement within the family. Our 11- and 12-year-old children were unsure what the next step was for them. (And I was unsure, too.) The local Casanova, it turned out, was 10 years old—and my two children were evidently feeling like 30-year-old virgins. Why had life passed them by? Were they sexually inadequate?

It was amusing, and instructive, to see how they and their friends organized to cope with the challenge. Over the next two or three weeks there were animated discussions among the boys and girls. It was interesting for me to note that although my son was already somewhat girl-shy, he was eager to discuss the situation with girls as well as boys. (After all, their opinion was important on this matter, too.) The culmination of the lengthy peer-group discussion was the decision to get a tape recorder and prepare a "documentary" of their feelings on the matter. The weight of opinion was against the young Casanova.

A further development in this situation was also helpful to the group. At their school, the teacher had invited students to bring in projects for discussion in class. The group played their tape in school—for a class in English! The teacher accepted this as a viable proposal and the entire class participated in a discussion of the problem. The ethos of the American school system accepts sex as a legitimate problem for discussion in the classroom. Notice that the tape was discussed not in a "sex education" class, but in an English class. The presence of sex education as an official part of the curriculum allows *other* classes and *other* teachers to take up questions relating to sex when they arise naturally in the course of events.

The crucial contribution of classes in sex education, or the discussion of problems in sexuality within the ordinary school curriculum, is that it ratifies the importance of boys and girls discussing their sexual questions and experiences *with one another*. What is actually taught or discussed in such classes is of far less importance than the fact that boys and girls talk about sex *with one another*. They come to learn about the feelings of the other sex. In this way, their fantasies and fears can be gradually dispelled and replaced by personal understanding. Most important of all, boys and girls can begin to realize something about the feeling of their potential partners—and something about their effect on themselves. Through talking, they come to understand the aspirations and anxieties of others. They can then let such understanding influence their own behavior so that they can become nonaggressive and kind.

From a psychoanalytic perspective, virginity is related to the status of maidenhood while coitus initiates a woman to the realm of mothers. We might recall our earlier discussion of the anxiety of the male before the sexual power of the female (symbolically the mother), an anxiety that threatened to render him impotent unless it could be transformed into aggression whereby he could dominate the female. By imagining her as hostile or potentially dangerous, the primitive male was able to generate the feeling of aggression required for phallic penetration. It was because the sexual relation drew upon this reservoir of anxiety and aggression that the premodern world regarded friendship between sexual partners as impossible. It was the historical contribution of late medieval courtly love to establish the new behavioral possibility of sexualized friendship. The American petting practice not only appropriates this contribution, but does so through methods that are very much the same as those developed by the courtly lovers themselves.

[Compare, for example, this description of the practice of courtly love with the American petting process. "Even in the final stage, the behavior of the [courtly] lover and his lady was, by most standards, curious, if not altogether improbable. For they were very likely to indulge repeatedly in protracted sessions of sex play, unclothed and in bed, without yielding to the imperious drive toward completion. . . . And scores of rhapsodists of *l'amour courtois* scorned the culmination of the sex act as false love while extolling as true love the pure kissing, touching, fondling, and naked contact of the lovers."[18] The courtly lovers were creating, in this way, a love that could endure sexual differences without falling prey to anxiety and aggression. Their self-confidence would develop from the gradual exploration and appreciation of sexual differences, an exploration that could be continued without danger precisely because the relation was to remain chaste.

Notice that in courtly love, as in the American petting process, virginity was a competence required of both men and women—because the pleasures sought were also fully mutual!]

The removal of aggression from the sexual relation has a remarkable effect on sexual roles. As long as sex is aggressive, each partner imagines the other to be radically different from himself. Once this aggression is removed, each partner is able to discover the other as a sexual *person*— as someone possessing feelings and imaginations that he himself can also share. As sexual love becomes tender and intimate, the man learns the woman's feelings and responses and the woman learns the man's. As they talk with each other about how they act, react, and interact, each can begin to incorporate, by empathetic imagination, the feelings of the other within his own range of behavioral possibilities. The man can begin to feel more "feminine," the woman more "masculine." As the motivation in sexual union ceases to be aggression and becomes the loving desire for communion, the sexual differences of the partners are softened and they become "psychologically bisexual."

The development of the ideal of personal friendship and intimacy as the determining feature of sexual love in America—an ideal inculcated through the petting process—means the breaking down of sexual interaction in terms of "roles." This ideal, and the heightened self-consciousness through which it is attained, reduces the tendency of the man to act like a "male" and the woman to act like a "female." Charles Winick in *The New People* has gathered massive data to document this breaking down of sexual role behavior in the United States and the emergence of a large number of people who, through heightened capacity for interpersonal empathy, share the same sexual feelings. Men and women today are becoming psychologically bisexual—*which means, as we shall see, that they are also becoming psychologically heterosexual.*

An interesting contemporary example of this psychological bisexuality is the complex image of man and woman presented in *Playboy* magazine. In the new symbol complex of the "Playboy-and-Playmate," several new trends in human sexuality are given expression. Of course, every sexual symbol contains elements of the past—and the Playboy-Playmate is no exception. In this magazine we find patriarchalism and the traditional exploitation of sexual anxiety that is found in every "girlie magazine." But to focus on these is to miss the important thing. What is important is what marks out a new sexual possibility.

What is especially unusual about the Playboy-Playmate symbolism is that the sexually attractive woman is here conceived as a friend and equal. The very name "Playmate" carries with it reminiscences of pre-adolescent childhood when sexual differences were not decisive for friendship groups. The "Playmate" is the girl from whom all the aggressive aspects of human sexuality have been removed. (Many commentators even call her asexual. They reveal their own male group bias!)

The Playmate is not of interest simply for her sexual functions alone. The photo montage that surrounds the Playmate portrays her in a variety of everyday activities: going to work, visiting her family, climbing mountains and sailing, dancing and dining out, figuring out her income tax. She is, first and foremost, the Playboy's all-day, all-night pal.

Playboy magazine is aimed at the college-aspiring group within our society, that is, at those persons who prolong adolescence while they learn specialized social and work skills. This prolongation of adolescence leads, as we have seen, to a greater integration of sexual and personal feeling and behavior. Those men and women who begin full sexual life immediately after the onset of puberty never attain to such an integration. For them, sex remains to a high degree segmental.

We can see this difference between the integrated sex of the upper middle class and the segmented sex of the lower middle class by comparing the *Playboy* symbol of man-and-woman with the parallel image of man-and-woman found in lower-middle-class "girlie magazines" (that is, in magazines aimed at a readership that has had a shorter adolescence and hence not learned the full integration of personal and sexual feelings).

The girl in lower-middle-class girlie magazines is never portrayed as a man's friend—and for neither her man nor for her is sex "just fun." Sex for them is always deadly serious. It is where they prove their manhood and their womanhood. This girl is always portrayed as a threat to the male. She is pictured with animal skins, boots, and a whip. She dresses in exotic black lace and various erotica. She is dangerous and bad. She poses a threat to the man who is not Male enough to take her. Her man is not some Playboy, but a real Male tested in deadly combat with his buddies (the girlie magazines are filled with tales of the muscular adventures of all male groups) and he knows how to tame her, too. He will "lay it on her" (how many men still talk this way?) and "make a woman out of her."

It is important to note how such a stress on sexual differences and aggressive sexuality leads to an almost exclusively homosexual organization of human life. The worlds of the Real Male and the Real Female (of the girlie magazines) remain totally separate. This Male and this Female have nothing in common except sex. This peculiar fact explains, I believe, why there is such deep anxiety about homosexuality in traditional patriarchal societies. It is because so much of the life in such societies is actually lived out in homosexual groups. Men and women never come to know each other, and hence cannot ever love each other. Friendship, to the extent that it exists in such societies, must be among persons of the same sex.

In contrast, the psychologically bisexual society (symbolized by *Playboy*) brings men and women into constant relation with each other so that all their activities are heterosexual. In fact, in the Playboy-Playmate symbol, there is no longer a "man's world" and a "woman's world." Space has become totally voluntarized. The Playmate likes mountain climbing, working for a living, and being independent. The Playboy likes to cook (he's a gourmet chef!), enjoys shopping for cosmetics and fashionable clothes (for himself!), and even is interested in playing "mother" to the kids. The Playboy LIKES children. Imagine that!

The equalitarian, nonaggressive relation between the Playboy and the Playmate stresses the similarity between the two. He enjoys sex, she enjoys sex. (It would be impossible to guess which is the aggressor.) And just as the Playmate is a passive sexual object for her man (the three-page nude photo for which the magazine is famous), so the Playboy is also a passive sexual object for his girl. Every issue of *Playboy* carries within it this ad, which asks: "What sort of a man reads *Playboy?*" And the accompanying photo shows a cute young man being guardedly ogled by some cute young woman. The assumption behind this set of images is that the man and the woman are both able to enjoy, and to manage, active and passive sexual roles.

The image of the Playboy-Playmate shows the extent to which psychological bisexuality has emerged within middle- and upper-middle-class America. There is nothing within this world that remains For Men Only or For Women Alone. But the most important thing to notice is how this psychological bisexuality actually means radical heterosexuality. It means that there is nothing in the woman's world that is absolutely alien to a man—and vice versa. The implication of this fact is that all social life can be heterosexual, that men and women can be constant companions and the best of friends. It means that their sexual relation will no longer be segmented from, but integrated within, their total personal life together.

CHAPTER VIII

Promiscuous Virgins

THE American petting process has been judged harshly from two points of view. Traditional Christian moralists regard it as a hypocritical compromise. They charge it with being a "technical evasion" of the strict claims put upon Christians for premarital chastity. From another viewpoint, traditional Freudians attack petting as a perversion. Freud, for example, argued that healthy genital sexuality aimed directly at coital orgasm, and that such sexual behavior as kissing was actually an unnatural detour from the chief purpose of the sexual act.[19] Many persons repeat this Freudian criticism, arguing that petting "fixates" people in pregenital sexuality so that they never are able to attain healthy adult orgasm.

The purpose of what follows is to consider certain of these claims. For if they are true, then it must be conceded that the fundamental mode of heterosexual learning and interaction in America is unnatural, perverse, and a moral hypocrisy. Let us, to begin, focus the question by considering the following observation of Harvey Cox: "Both the romantic ideal and the identification of intercourse with coitus are cultural accretions that have coalesced with the rule of premarital chastity. . . . The ideal of romantic love is the most obvious mythical excrescence. It leads often to the belief that certain forms of intimacy become progressively less objectionable the more you 'love' the boy. . . .

"A more stubborn and deceptive segment of folklore that has been equated with the doctrine of premarital chastity is one that is rarely discussed openly: the curious presumption that a person who has not experienced coital intercourse remains a virgin—no matter what else he or she has done. . . .

"[For example] a pert young graduate of a denominational college assured me recently that although she had necked to orgasm every weekend for two years, she had 'never gone all the way.' Her 'premarital chastity' was intact.

"Or was it? Only, I submit, by the most technical definition of what it means to preserve virginity."[20]

Cox's criticism shows that he feels there is a kind of self-contradiction involved in the coed's petting. She both wants and doesn't want sex. That is, she seeks both to maintain her virginity and to attain sexual gratification. Cox describes her behavior as "promiscuous virginity" and "non-coital promiscuity." If, says Cox, the girl who pets to orgasm insists she is still a virgin, she is making a mere technical distinction. She is but a "technical virgin."

Cox's suggestion that persons who engage in petting are making "technical"—but not "real"—distinctions implies that he knows what *natural* sexual behavior is. His criticism resembles the Catholic argument against contraception: that such a practice introduces an "artificial" distinction into a natural process and thereby distorts it from its real end. But what Cox and Catholics—and Sigmund Freud himself—are doing is to elevate a form of sexual experience characteristic of a particular stage of cultural evolution into a description of the essence of sexuality itself. They judge that forms of sexual behavior that do not correspond with their notion of what is natural must be artificial and wrong. They are philosophical realists who assume that "virginity," "coitus," and "perversion" are determinate entities or essences that can be given transcultural definition. It is hard to see why we should agree. Rather, it would seem that every conception of a sexual "unit"—for example, every definition of "virginity" or "coitus"—is a cultural definition. It expresses the view of the sexual process characteristic of a certain evolutionary stage.

It may make sense to assume there is some foundational sexual nature in man, but it is difficult to understand how we could ever know it or make use of this concept, since genital competence is present only in humans who are elaborately socialized, and sexual intercourse is an activity that cultures always limit, shape, and steer. The conceptual units or definitions that we *assume* to be foundational, or natural, are therefore always expressive of a certain cultural outlook. Even scientific studies of human sexual behavior by Kinsey, Masters/Johnson, and others do not describe the sexual behavior of man in general, but rather present abstractions from the sexual behavior of *particular humans*—whose sexual responses are determined by their culture. Such scientific studies are important, and, within our own culture, socially useful. But they do not give us the "real" truth about sex. Such scientific conclusions, which seek to explode cultural assumptions about sex, are as much the expressions of a cultural orientation as the assumptions they attack.

The way a man conceptually unitizes the sexual process, i.e., the units he assumes to be real or natural rather than distasteful or conventional, tells us more about his understanding of human sexuality than all the things he subsequently says about these units. Hence, we should recall that just as some today question the possibility or legitimacy of differentiating coitus and petting to orgasm, so at other times and places it has also been thought to be impossible or improper (a) to differentiate a private relation between a man and a woman from a sexual relation, (b) to differentiate the manual examination of the vagina by a male physician from phallic penetration and (c) to differentiate a volition from a bodily action ("He who looks upon a woman with lust in his heart has *already* . . ."). And in a classic case of pastoral counseling, St. Augustine even had to reassure a group of violated Christian nuns that there really is a difference between being raped and consenting to sexual union. The essence of sexual union, he argued, is the mutual voluntary consent of the two parties to each other in and through the act itself.

The nuns—at least some of them—were not sure Augustine was right. Perhaps he was only making a "technical distinction." How can one be sure that the "essence" of sexual union is the mutual voluntary consent of the two parties to each other—rather than the mere physical penetration of the vagina by the penis? In fact, when Augustine made his argument, he *was* innovating a new conception of sexual union. Before early Christianity and the conception of man as a free spiritual being, the essence of every human action was always identified with the physical expression of that act. Before early Christianity, man experienced himself essentially as a body rather than as a soul. This meant that he had to understand sexual intercourse in terms of the physical act of penetration. Why else, for example, the primitive preoccupation with the preservation of an intact hymen for the wedding night?

To be able to define the essence of sexual union as mutual voluntary consent presupposes that man has begun to experience himself as a free, spiritual being. From the point of view of a person who experiences himself essentially as a body, the definition of the essence of sexual union as mutual voluntary consent seems like an equivocation, a mere "technical distinction" that has no basis in reality. But from the point of view of a person who experiences himself as essentially a free, or spiritual, being, the definition of sexual intercourse as a physical union that merely *expresses* the real voluntary union, or mutual commitment, of the partners to each other is the only definition that makes sense. For the person who experiences himself as essentially a voluntary being, genital contact that is not the expression of personal consent is as little a union with another as being bumped against another person in a New York subway.

[It is, perhaps, important to point out that once we have experienced man (i.e., ourselves) as an essentially free, or voluntary, being, we can no longer accept the traditional judgment that all sexual intercourse within marriage is moral while all sexual intercourse outside marriage is not. For two persons to be married does not make their intercourse moral unless in *every specific act* of sexual union both partners are freely choosing to give themselves to each other. Too many times marital sex is not such a voluntary and personal self-giving. It is far too often something that one does or yields to out of a sense of obligation or out of a one-sided physical tension and need. It is too often a form of aggression and domination by the man or manipulation and control by the woman. In such cases, sexual intercourse is intrinsically immoral—given the experience of man as a free, spiritual being. The mere fact that such "obligatory" intercourse takes place within marriage does not remove it from the category of rape. And such marital rape is a far more serious violation of the dignity of persons than is any nonmarital intercourse that is undertaken by two partners in full mutual love and consent. Some will feel, of course, that such considerations rest too much on "technical distinctions" (e.g., the spiritual character of man) and are really in violation of the "nature" of marriage. But they raise the question: What kind of a being is man? And what does this mean for his sexual life?]

The evolution of sexuality, as an expression of the evolution of human consciousness, is man's learning to reconstruct his sexual behavior in order to express his ever-more complex sense of self. Such a reconstruction involves the introducing of new distinctions into sexual behavior—new distinctions that will, from the point of view of earlier stages of development, be regarded as "technical" rather than "real." But such differentiations presuppose the emergence in man of a sense of his own freedom. They presuppose the development of abstractive intelligence that is capable of making a distinction, or drawing a line, in the intellectual and moral order even where one cannot be seen in the physical world. It may not seem, from the physical point of view, that there is much difference between petting to orgasm and sexual intercourse. It may not seem, from the physical point of view, that a girl who pets to orgasm still remains a virgin. But such a distinction does make sense in the intellectual and moral order. It is a way man has of imposing his own meanings upon the physical world and integrating his instinctual and voluntary behavior.

Even more important than the ability to make such intellectual distinctions is the psychological competence to operate in terms of such "invisible lines." To do so, as the young coed did, is to live as a spiritual, or intellectual, being. It is to define oneself symbolically, in terms of free choice. It is to resist the regressive tendency to deny or blur such "invisible lines" in order to recover a simpler, physical world. The ability to

operate in terms of such distinctions has not been sufficiently appreciated. To make an intellectual distinction requires, after all, the
psychological power to sustain an inner tension; and to act on the basis
of this distinction requires the further psychological strength to operate
in terms of a more complex world. The ability to continue petting, to
make precise distinctions in sexual behavior, without demanding *either*
the renunciation of all sexual intimacy *or* "coitus now!" is the same
ability as that required to maintain the intellectual investigation of a
problem without demanding a premature resolution. Note that in both
the sexual and the intellectual orders what is at stake is the ability to
expose oneself to a problematic reality, to endure the tension of contrary
feelings and questions, while bearing the anxiety that such openness
involves—resisting the urge toward closure.

These considerations help us to understand why, from studies of the
sexual behavior of many American men and women, we find a correla-
tion between the length of formal education and the length of time
virginity has been maintained (and petting has been practiced). The
longer virginity is maintained, the more time adolescents have to learn
the multiple discriminations required to attain to full personal-sexual
intimacy. To learn these discriminations requires the development of
abstractive intelligence, the ability to think of oneself as a rational and
free being, and the attainment of a capacity for heterosexual equality and
openness. The psychological competences that undergird such a growth
in sexual behavior are precisely the same competences used to do successful work in relatively abstract fields of study in a university. Hence, we
find that those persons who go on to universities *also* begin their adult
sexual life relatively later than those who do not. They spend more time
being adolescents.

On the other hand, those persons who begin regular sexual intercourse
soon after puberty never go through such a learning process and never
develop such a highly differentiated sexual behavior. They are, for example, less likely to engage in lengthy foreplay before an act of intercourse,
less likely to extend the period of coital union, and less inclined to engage
in expression of affection outside the bedroom. Moreover, as we shall see

in the next section, they are less inclined to accept equalitarian relations between men and women.

The psychological competences presupposed by, and developed through, the petting process are precisely those abstractive and voluntary competences that are involved in intellectual development and moral growth. The capacity to maintain virginity is, therefore, an important element in the attainment of the kind of maturity related to romantic-personal marriage and democratic society. Precocious coitus, for this reason, is not simply "immoral," but also socially dysfunctional. For example, at age 12 only 1.1% of those men who eventually attended college had experienced premarital intercourse compared with 10.8% of those men whose education did not continue beyond the eighth grade. Correlations for other ages are as follows:[21]

AGE	ATTENDED COLLEGE	EIGHTH GRADE OR LESS
14	5.9%	34.8%
16	15.6	66.8
18	31.4	81.9
20	45.5	86.6
22	55.8	87.9
25	65.9	88.9

Note that at age 18, ordinarily the first year of college, only ⅓ of the college males had experienced premarital intercourse compared with over ⁴⁄₅ of those males whose education did not continue beyond the eighth grade. The lengthier period of virginity for the college group is coupled with their development of more differentiated sexual behavior. Other studies, furthermore, have shown that within this group (including, of course, both men and women) there is more petting, more foreplay, more integration of personal and sexual feeling, and—contrary to pornographic imagination!—more sexual satisfaction.

We shall now consider how the petting process—and the concomitant extension of the period of virginity—finally leads to a change in the moral standards by which people judge their sexual behavior. The crucial point to notice is that the process of graduated intimacy involved in petting not only leads finally to sexual intercourse (even premarital sexual intercourse), but also gradually changes the moral standards of those involved so that they accept this outcome as right and proper. Among those groups of persons who do not pet, the double standard prevails. But among persons who do pet, there is mutual acceptance of a single standard morality that legitimates intercourse for both men and women.

How does the petting process change moral standards? It does so, I suggest, by gradually replacing institutional legitimations for sexual intimacy with personal ones. It does so by inculcating a moral feeling or attitude that allows sexual affection to be expressed in a degree proportional to the degree of love (friendship) existing between the parties. I want, at this point, to stress that this principle does *not* legitimate sexual union among young adolescents, because young adolescents are not able to love in a fully voluntary and mutual way. The process of sexual learning that takes place in petting is *also* a process of learning to love. That is, in petting, persons learn not simply the mechanics of sex, but also the psychological difficulties and personal strengths involved in loving.

Throughout this book, we have seen that if the goal of the sexual process is to be full mutuality, the partners must be fully open and equally responsive to each other. Without equality, openness, and co-initiative the goal of shared communion cannot be attained. Hence, built into the structure of the petting process is a bias toward the equalization of the partners and the encouragement that each seek to be and do what the other wants. Sexual intercourse is finally also assimilated within the petting process. The same consideration (behavior proportionate to degree of mutual affection) that legitimates light caresses will eventually also legitimate coitus. To add intercourse as an eventual outcome does not, of course, destroy the *gradualness* of the petting process, but does allow that, after the partners are sufficiently mature and capable of committed love, premarital intercourse is a proper next step. The *age* at which persons arrive at this maturity will vary, of course. But it would appear that, according to present practices, it might fall toward the end of adolescence, that is, within the late college years.

[A characteristically American argument and judgment on this point has been made by Rustum and Della Roy. After arguing for the moral acceptability of premarital intercourse on the principle that it might be an act proportionate to the degree of intimacy between a couple, they then go on to observe:

"It behooves us also to report why the possibility of premarital coitus being the best choice for late-teen couples appears to us, on the basis of empirical evidence, to be the exception rather than the rule. The most important reason is that intercourse, especially regular premarital intercourse, can inhibit rather than aid the deepening of a relationship in the formative stages. . . . In *typical* middle-class America, then, the most advanced stage of college and late high school premarital sexual activity would be mutual petting to orgasm, which would serve both as the expression of caring in a deep relationship combined with alleviation of part of the sexual tension resulting from our highly eroticized culture. Such a limitation in most cases fits in with the intention of keeping the sexual expression of a relationship *below* the appropriate level for periods of several months to a year or so, which appears to be within the realm of possibility for the majority of Americans.

"Value is still seen in the sublimation made possible by some degree of self-denial, which is almost essential during the formative years, when personality growth, development of social responsibility, study and hard work for the future are the primary concerns of the person. If it is claimed that such attempted sublimation in our overly sexually stimulated climate causes more distraction from concentrated hard work than would regular intercourse, we would still interject the idea of a *gradual* escalation of intimacy. As the acceptance of the rightness of other forms of sexual expression goes further (especially also of the role of masturbation) many deep relationships need not go beyond petting to orgasm. A quality of difference, then, is yet seen between even such a highly advanced mode of sexual expression and coitus, which could be reserved for a marital or near marital relationship."[22]]

Contrary to much of the popular press, it is not the easy availability of the contraceptive pill that has changed premarital sexual behavior. The general acceptance of premarital intercourse as a part of the petting process dates back to that generation of men and women who were teenagers during the First World War. Whereas at the turn of the century only 14% of American women engaged in premarital sexual intercourse, by the 1920s the figure had risen to 50%—a figure that compares roughly to the present sexual experience of, say, Oberlin College coeds. Moreover, during this same two-decade period, there was a sharp *decrease* in the number of males who avoided premarital intercourse with their fiancées, but engaged in intercourse "with others only." This shows that men began giving up their "double standard" attitudes. That is, they ceased condemning women for engaging in the same premarital intercourse that they engaged in themselves. These figures can be seen in the following table showing incidence of premarital coitus.[23]

	DECADE OF BIRTH		
	before 1890	1890–1899	1900–1909
Husbands			
None	50.6%	41.9%	32.6%
With fiancée only	4.6	7.6	17.2
With fiancée and others	9.2	23.0	33.7
With others only	35.6	27.5	16.5
Wives			
None	86.5	74.0	51.2
With fiancé only	8.7	17.7	32.7
With fiancé and others	2.9	5.8	14.0
With others only	1.9	2.5	2.1

The sharp decrease in the number of American men having premarital intercourse "with others only" shows the social phasing out of segmental "body-centered coitus"—or sex where there is no deep affection or commitment to the other *person*. It shows also the increased acceptance of a single-standard morality that legitimates premarital intercourse for *both the man and the woman* under conditions of mutual love and commitment.

The sociologist Ira Reiss has learned that the "single standard" morality which legitimates premarital sex as an expression of mutual love is found only among "the college educated segments of our society."[24] Among the noncollege educated groups of our society, the attitudes toward premarital intercourse remain either "double standard" (taboo for women) or "prohibition" (taboo for both).

Reiss has found the following attitudes toward premarital coitus among various American groups: (1) The Double Standard, (2) Prohibition, (3) Permissiveness Without Affection (e.g., segmental "body-centered" coitus as with prostitutes), and (4) Permissiveness With Affection. Permissiveness With Affection is the attitude that condones sexual intercourse for two persons if they love each other and are mature enough to express their love through this act (i.e., integrative personal-sexual intercourse). This kind of coitus is "person-centered" (as distinguished from "body-centered"). Person-centered coitus involves the integration of moral and instinctual feelings; body-centered coitus assumes their separation and segmentalization. Person-centered coitus uses sex only as an expression of love, esteem, and commitment; body-centered coitus uses sex for segmentalized body pleasure and can say "But, of course, he/she didn't really mean anything to me." The former uses sex as the expression of a relation; the latter uses sex simply for orgasm and tension release.

To manage person-centered, or integrative, sex requires a great deal of psychosocial skill. It would, therefore, not be surprising that this person-centered coitus will be found in those segments of our society that put greater stress upon the development of autonomous identity, self-possession, and the priority of personhood over sexual role. And this is what Reiss' studies show: that such integrative sex is found among the college segments of our society. (The college group is also characterized by its smaller number of Permissiveness Without Affection adherents.) Thus it seems, says Reiss, that the standard of "Permissiveness With Affection is likely stronger at the middle- and upper-middle-class levels, while Permissiveness Without Affection is stronger in other parts of our society."[25] Reiss concludes with the observation that the length of education—hence, the length of adolescence—seems more "strongly predictive of sexual behavior than other factors such as religion."[26]

[The attitudes toward sexual behavior Reiss has found do roughly correspond to the three cultures we have previously considered. (1) The Double Standard and Permissiveness Without Affection are characteristic of the covenantal-legal, or patriarchal. (2) The Prohibition is characteristic of the early and Catholic Christian. (3) The standard of Permissiveness With Affection is characteristic of the spiritualistic-individualistic.]

It should be pointed out that, while sexual attitudes may be better predicted on the basis of education than religion, it is also true that different religious groups have different attitudes toward education—especially education for women. The high valuation of education for *all* persons is characteristic of American culture. The tendency of our culture is to prolong the period of adolescence and education in order to maximize possibilities for a person to break with parental identity and to choose the form of his own adulthood. Without this emphasis on education, neither the individualism nor the spiritualistic reconstruction of nature and human nature by the power of technology would be possible.

When we consider that, since the First World War, the number of Americans in the prolonged adolescence, or college, group has rapidly increased, we can see why the number of persons adhering to the Permissiveness With Affection standard of sexual behavior is also rapidly increasing. The percentage of Americans in the college-age group who actually attend college has risen from 17% in the 1920s to 30% by the late 1950s to well over 50% in the 1970s. If all other factors remain the same, this will mean that the Permissiveness With Affection standard of sexual behavior will become, or already has become, the accepted standard of sexual behavior for the majority of Americans. And it will mean, also, that Prohibition and the Double Standard will become increasingly dysfunctional as moral guides for the sexual behavior of youth.

The emergence of a new moral standard for sexual love implies, also, the emergence of a new experience of sexual love. It is hard for us to understand this because it is a notion that runs contrary to all traditional expectations. But persons who operate with a single standard (Permissiveness With Affection) morality also experience sexual desire differently than do persons who operate with a Double Standard morality. Persons who operate with a Permissiveness With Affection morality feel their sexual desire as a desire for communion. They experience sexual desire as a seeking to be identified with another person. Persons who operate with a Double Standard morality experience sexual desire not as a desire for communion, but as a desire for private sexual orgasm or tension release. They experience it in terms of aggression and domination, perhaps. But not as a desire for full interpersonal sharing.

Before it is integrated within the total personality, sexual desire is experienced as *eros*—as a drive that is discontinuous with moral feeling, as a biological need or hunger. An example of such eros love is seen in current music where the man sings "I want you, I need you, I love you. . . ." In his experience, to "want," to "need," and to "love" all mean the same thing. This man's love is an eros love. It is not a love for another person. It is, rather, a desire to use another person to complete, or compensate for, a lack in himself. It is a passion that arises out of a need. Such love is, inevitably, self-centered. The person who is filled with needs can never experience another person as anything other than a completion of these needs. He cannot really see the other as a person or love that other person as a friend.

Another example: a *Cosmopolitan* magazine description of the perfect Latin lover. "When a Latin lover says 'I love you,' he is really saying that he needs you and has to have you." To say "I love you" in this situation means nothing more than "I want to take you to bed." For a woman to find a man who "needs" her and is unable to overcome this need without taking her to bed is, of course, a very safe thing. The woman is safe with such a man because he cannot do without her. But he never loves her for what she is in herself. Hence, she is "functionalized." She exists for the man only insofar as he has this need—and many women prefer to be sexually needed in just this way rather than to be loved as free and independent persons.

It should be clear that the love or affection that legitimates sexual intercourse in terms of the standard Permissiveness With Affection is not this kind of eros love. For eros love is not an affection for *another person*.

It is, rather, a disguised love for oneself—since it desires the other person only to the degree that the other person fulfills one's own needs. Such eros love is, therefore, a biological appetite that is discontinuous with volition and friendship. As such, it cannot contain within itself the moral criterion for any act. A moral criterion has to refer to human consciousness and will. Where sexual desire has not been moralized and integrated within the whole of personal awareness and volition, such sexual desire cannot be a moral justification for sexual relations. If a person experiences sex as an uncontrollable need or appetite, then it is a contradiction in terms for him to speak of his intercourse as a way of communing, or communicating, with someone else. For communicative sex presupposes that sex functions as an instrument of personal volition (i.e., that sex is person-centered rather than body-centered). Eros love, however, never experiences sex as an instrument of the volition, but rather as an autonomous drive that is segmented off from the rest of the personality.

Wherever sexual desire is experienced as this autonomous, or segmented, need or drive, it is inevitably the case that sex will be controlled by standards extrinsic to itself. Usually this means that some rational or legal consideration is introduced to provide moral legitimation for intercourse. For example, those who argue that "marriage" must be introduced to moralize the sexual relation and protect the partners from mutual exploitation frequently suppose that sexual "love" is a nonvoluntary biological appetite.

However, once sexual love has been moralized and integrated within the total personality structure, then it is no longer a purely biological appetite that must be controlled by reference to extrinsic criteria. Once sexual love has been integrated with personal love, so that what one loves sexually is the other *person* and that person's good, then this love can itself provide intrinsic criteria determining when and where intercourse may take place. For example, let us suppose that sexual desire has been moralized. Let us suppose that this sexual desire is no longer simply a need for orgasm, a private grasping for satisfaction, a hunting after "outlets." Let us suppose that sexual desire has become a desire for increased intimacy and communion with another, an expression of deepest friendship. Let us suppose that one seeks, through a sexual relation, not his own satisfaction and private orgasm, but the joy of perfect sharing. Such sexual desire is a totally different thing from eros love. It is an "agapic-love," or a love that finds joy not in the fulfillment of one's private needs, but rather in the heightened communion with, and contemplation of, another. It is a love that finds happiness in the act of sharing.

Such an "agapic-love" presupposes that the instinctual "need" component of sex (that is always self-centered) has been overcome so that man's desire has been turned outward toward another. It presupposes that sexual desire is no longer autoerotic (that is, seeking to satisfy *oneself*), but heteroerotic (that is, seeking to enjoy and unite with *another*). It presupposes that sexual desire aims not at orgasm, but at mutuality and sharing.

It is important to realize that the preoccupation with orgasm as the goal of sexual intercourse reveals a failure to develop beyond autosexuality into the full maturity of heterosexuality. Preoccupation with orgasm as the goal of intercourse is preoccupation with oneself and one's need for private tension release. An example of precisely such a preoccupation with orgasm is found in the work of Masters and Johnson. Having identified orgasm as the goal of the sexual act, they then proceed to see no essential difference between masturbation and intercourse as effective sexual outlets. In their conclusion they are consistent, though mistaken in their original assumption. If the goal of sexual activity is orgasm, then they are correct in seeing no essential difference between masturbation and intercourse—for then intercourse will be nothing essentially more than masturbation *à deux*. But such intercourse is merely a disguised form of autosexuality. The mere presence of another person in the bed while one is having an orgasm does not make one's sexual activity heterosexual. *A sexual union is heterosexual only if the presence of the other person is intrinsically related to the goal of the sexual act itself.* This means that only as sexual desire aims at communion rather than orgasm is sexual intercourse a heterosexual activity.

Once sexual love is experienced as a will for intimate mutual communion, this love is capable of providing the intrinsic moral criteria justifying sexual intimacies and intercourse. For in such a desire for communion, there is a certain objectivity about the other and his happiness and total life. It is a love (that is, an intelligent awareness, identification with, and will for the good of another) that is able to think and to choose. To suggest that sexual love can never attain this degree of objectivity and intelligence is to accept the inevitability of a segmentation of the instinctual and the moral realms. And to accept such a segmentation will finally inhibit in persons the development of their capacity for personal unitive love.

What persons must do is to learn to love each other as friends, integrating moral and sexual feelings so perfectly that they are capable of letting love and that love alone guide their behavior. Friends do not constantly look for external criteria to govern their behavior. What they do grows out of their desire for increased communion, their desire to receive each other into their own lives so that each may be greater than either is alone. Such a love seeks the good of both of them and the continuation of their love. Only if persons learn to love sexually in this way—rather than falling back into eros love and extrinsic justifications for intercourse—will they attain to the fullest possibilities that are open to man and woman.

[The new experience of sexual desire as a unitive love, or spiritual passion, came into the West with courtly love. But there are marked similarities between this unitive love and certain Oriental ideals of sexuality. For example, consider Alan Watts' following description of *maithuna*.

"As we have seen, the problems of sexuality cannot be solved on their own level. . . . To serve as a means of initiation to the 'one body' of the universe, it requires what we have called a contemplative approach. This is not love 'without desire' in the sense of love without delight, but love which is not contrived or wilfully provoked as an escape from the habitual empty feeling of an isolated ego.

"It is not quite correct to say that such a relationship goes far beyond the 'merely sexual,' for it would be better to say that sexual contact irradiates every aspect of the encounter, spreading its warmth into work and conversation outside the bounds of actual 'love-making.' Sexuality is not a separate compartment of human life; it is a radiance pervading every human relationship, but assuming a particular intensity at certain points. Conversely, we might say that sexuality is a special mode or degree of total intercourse of man and nature."

In this conception of a sexual desire transformed by being lifted from a limited "genital segment" into the totality of personal expression, Watts shows certain parallels between *maithuna* and that tendency toward the integration of the rational and the sexual beginning at the second axial period. He goes on to say:

"Sexual love in the contemplative spirit simply provides the conditions in which we can be aware of our mutual interdependence and 'oneness.' The point is so important that it can bear repetition: contemplative love—like contemplative meditation—is only quite secondarily a matter of technique. For it has no specific aim; there is nothing particular that has to be made to happen [e.g., it does *not* purposefully aim at orgasm]. It is simply that a man and a woman are together exploring their spontaneous feeling—without any preconceived idea of what it ought to be, since the sphere of contemplation is not what should be, but what is. . . . One of the first phases of contemplative love is the discovery of the depth and satisfaction of very simple contacts which are ordinarily called 'preliminaries' to sexual activity. But in a relationship which has no goal other than itself, nothing is merely preliminary. One finds out what it can mean simply to look at the other person, to touch hands, or listen to the voice. . . .

"As the lead and response of good dancers appears to be almost simultaneous, as if they were a single entity, there comes a moment when more intimate sexual contact occurs with extraordinary mutuality. The man does not lead and the woman follow; the man-and-woman relationship acts of itself. The feeling of this mutuality is entirely distinct from that of a man initiating sexual contact with a perfectly willing woman. His 'advance' and her 'response' seems to be the *same* moment. . . .

"The psychic counterpart of this bodily and sensuous intimacy is a similar openness of attention to each other's thoughts—a form of communion which can be as sexually 'charged' as physical contact. This is the feeling that one can express one's thoughts to the other just as they are, since there is not the slightest compulsion to assume a pretended character. This is perhaps the rarest and most difficult aspect of any human relationship. . . . Yet this is quite the most important part of a deep sexual relationship, and it is in some way understood even when thoughts are left unsaid. . . . To unveil the flow of thought can therefore be an even greater sexual intimacy than physical nakedness."

Notice the resemblances to the romantic ideal and the petting process.]

CHAPTER IX

Benjamin Graduates

SEXUAL love between persons that aims primarily at communion is different from sexual desire that aims primarily at private orgasm. Sexual *love* presupposes the evolution of consciousness into self-consciousness. It presupposes that a man experiences himself and others as free spiritual beings with feelings, thoughts, and aspirations that mark each man as unlike every other man. What is sought in the communion of sexual love, then, is intimacy—the opening of one soul to another, the mutual sharing of innermost life.

In pre-biblical times, when human beings experienced themselves primarily as bodies rather than as self-conscious free spirits, the highest conceivable mode of union between humans was also thought to be bodily union. Hence, the metaphor for sexual union (also carried over into the Bible) is that through intercourse men become "one flesh." Once human beings become self-conscious, an alternative notion of true personal union begins to emerge. Men begin to seek spiritual communion. They seek, through love, to become "one spirit." Only as sexual intercourse is taken up into and made expressive of this spiritual communion is it now experienced as meaningful.

Yet personal communion requires the capacity of persons to open themselves to each other and to reveal the uniqueness of themselves as persons. This opening creates a unique intimacy, or nearness, of persons with each other. This intimacy is not a given. It is a spiritual, or free, creation. It exists only through a mutual voluntary act. It exists as one reality that expresses two persons' simultaneous opening themselves to each other. It exists not as a giving nor as a receiving, but as a *perfect sharing*. It takes co-initiative and co-responsiveness.

Intimacy is one of the highest and most difficult accomplishments of the human spirit. It is a spiritual act; two persons open themselves and enter into each other. They experience themselves as one. This spiritual communion is a much more intimate intercourse than mere genital intercourse. Hence, to "intimize" genital intercourse, it must be taken up into this unitive love. Sex must be integrated with love. Sexual desire must become the desire for the union and oneness of persons in their totality: soul and body.

It is clear that when this has occurred, sexual desire is transformed into a love that is totally different from the primal sexual aggression— the teasing and taking—that has not yet been moralized. In fact, sexual aggression is a cover for an absence of personal identity. Sexual aggression exists only where the beings involved do not experience themselves and others as persons, but only as sexual functions. The sexual behavior of animals is aggressive, i.e., functional. Animals are not persons, but are functions of their sexuality. The action of an animal is always an expression of the instinctual drives that ensure the survival of the species. In human beings, however, there is the possibility of a growth to personhood. This growth involves the emergence of intelligence and freedom, plus the use of that freedom to constitute oneself a unique being.

While it may be the case that, prior to the emergence of personhood, every male is like every other male and every female like every other female, this is not true after personhood has been developed. When beings are unique, when they are persons, the desire for sexual union with another's body can no longer be a desire to procreate a species or a mere desire for private orgasm. Rather, desire for sexual union with the body of a unique person is a desire to know him/her as a person more fully. The growth of personhood, the uniqueness of persons, implies a different kind of sexual love: one that aims at maximizing intimacy and sharing.

Because of its demands that a person be open and capable of sharing himself, intimacy is the most difficult and threatening of human acts. If a person has no sense of his own uniqueness, no identity which he experiences as his alone, then he cannot endure intimacy. This is because intimacy is a communion of persons, a communion that lies beyond every social role. If a person understands his identity only in terms of various social roles, he cannot manage intimacy. If he does not experience himself except in terms of others' expectations, he cannot be a true friend. For such persons, intimacy will be a disorienting, even a disintegrative, experience. The human being who is not fully a person must play roles, must be "Male" or "Female" in bed.

Awareness of oneself as a person transcending a sexual role is the hardest of insights to gain. It is easier, far easier, to become aware of the distinction between oneself and one's family, oneself and one's job, and oneself and one's religious beliefs. But to become aware of the distinction between one's uniqueness as a person and the sexual characteristics of one's body involves a radically heightened form of self-consciousness. This is the case even in modern societies.

One of the many educational methods now being used to help people learn what intimacy involves is the sensitivity group. But many people find such sensitivity groups a threat. They find the groups disorienting, upsetting their sense of self. Why is this the case? It is because in a sensitivity group, people discover their lack of personal identity, their lack of self-awareness. They learn the extent to which they have thought of themselves only in terms of the expectations of other people. They find that they do not know themselves, that they are visitors within their own bodies. The intimacy of the sensitivity group breaks the *persona*—the social mask, or "role"—that such alienated persons have been wearing throughout their lives. But this disintegration of the *persona*, or social front, can open the way for a new awareness of themselves as unique persons.

[A basic principle of metapsychology is that people can perceive in others only what they also experience in themselves. All interpersonal experience involves the projection of the form of one's own sense of selfhood upon others. A person who experiences himself as dependent projects this experience on others and denies that anyone else can be self-dependent. In the same way, only a person who experiences himself as unique can perceive the uniqueness of others. Ability to experience others requires, therefore, growth in oneself. Without this growth, there can be no experience of human beings as persons, but only as bundles of drives and social roles.]

Growth into personhood is not simply a growth that has taken place over the many centuries of human evolution, but it is a growth that has to take place in each individual human. Growing to adulthood involves learning those competences characteristic of one's culture. This means that every modern man must either recapitulate in his life, or otherwise learn and appropriate, the various stages of evolutionary process.

An American boy will go through a stage of experiencing sex as an instinctual eros. But, to become fully mature in terms of his own culture, he must grow beyond this eros-love (instinctual sexuality) and become competent in communitive love and friendship. To do this, he must become a unique person. He must separate himself from his family and biological identity, gradually gaining the ability to be self-dependent and free. Only after he has done this will he be able to love in an intimate way, for only persons have the power of intimacy; and "personhood" is not a given, but a difficult psychosocial achievement.

These considerations help us understand a second reason for the graduated character of the petting process. This process of gradual learning of psychosexual intimacy not only involves learning sexual technique, but also involves the growth toward personhood. The adolescent, still growing toward fullness of personhood, is not yet in a position to manage the fullest sexual mutuality and intimacy. He can share only as much as he already is, but he is not yet all that he will become. Erik Erikson says that adolescents cannot "love in that binding manner which only two identities can offer each other"—since their full personal identities have not yet been formed.[28]

[Erikson observes that "there are many forms of love from the infant's comfortable and anxious attachment to his mother to the adolescent's passionate and desperate infatuation, but love in the evolutionary and generational sense is, I believe, the transformation of the love received throughout the preadolescent stage of life into the care given to others during adult life. It must be an important evolutionary fact that man, over and above sexuality, develops a selectivity of love: I think it is the *mutuality of mates and partners in a shared identity.* . . . For let me emphasize here that identity proves itself strongest where it can take chances with itself. For this reason love in its truest sense presupposes both identity and fidelity."[29]]

The growth to autonomous personhood requires, first and foremost, gaining the power to remain faithful to oneself. Faithfulness, it should be stressed, is not simply a matter of faithfulness to others, but first of all a matter of faithfulness to oneself—a power to define oneself from within and to remain constant to that self-definition. In the last analysis, faithfulness is the power of personhood because it is a principle of order that is rooted in an individual man himself. By this power, a person can create the *logos,* or form, of his own life and become unique.

The development of personhood, especially this power of fidelity, is a fundamental problem for adolescents since this fidelity lays the basis for an adult communion and "sharing love." In Erik Erikson's attempt to chart the stages of growth to modern personhood, the development of the power of fidelity is seen to be the *primary* task of adolescence. He suggests that the various virtues, or character strengths, emerge in the following order:

1. hope	}	
2. will	}	childhood
3. purpose	}	
4. competence	}	
5. fidelity	}	adolescence
6. sharing love	}	
7. care	}	
8. wisdom	}	adulthood

In our previous discussion of the petting process, we have considered the development of *competence* in personal-sexual integration—the fourth of Erikson's virtues. But the petting process also assists in the development of fidelity (the fifth virtue) by encouraging persons to engage in limited, though progressively more intimate and involving, commitments. In this way the adolescent explores the meaning of fidelity, learning to commit himself and be committed. In fact, not only within the petting process, but also within the whole pattern of adolescent dating, there are relatively formalized "degrees of commitment." Group dating, dating *à deux*, going steady, "pinning," and even the American engagement (which is much more tentative than a European engagement) encourage the exploration of the meaning of human fidelity by allowing the adolescent to commit himself in many limited ways. In the course of this learning-behavior he gradually learns how to commit himself *fully* to a personal-romantic marriage and to a permanent adult career and identity.

In both traditional and American societies, there is a congruence between the methods of sexual initiation and initiation to an adult identity. A traditional society initiates by *bestowal:* the elders teach the youth and certify their competence. A modern society initiates by *experimentation:* a youth explores a variety of experiences and then chooses his own adulthood. In traditional societies, parents arrange the marriages of children for them. In America, youths gain sexual experience through the petting process and, on the basis of experience gained through this process, choose their own mates. The American adolescent chooses his adult career in the same way: by exploring a variety of fields and interests in order to learn what he can do and wants to do—and then choosing this.

Just as, in American society, the period of adolescence is regarded as a "moratorium" during which youths may change schools, jobs, fields, and interests without being charged with irresponsibility, so too is the petting process a kind of "moratorium." The similarity between the American method of choosing an adult vocation and the American method of gaining sexual maturity is of utmost importance. For it shows that the two processes are consistent, each reinforcing the other.

In traditional societies, there is congruence of methods for developing both career and sexual competences. The same adults who define the values and prescribe the careers proper to adolescents also introduce them into sexual adulthood and interpret the meaning of human sexuality for them. It should be noted that in a traditional society adults are as certain that they know the proper conditions and meaning of human sexual behavior in the lives of youth as they are certain they can choose satisfying adult careers for them. Contrast this traditional certainty with the confession of the typical American parent that he "does not know" what to advise his teenage children with respect to sexual behavior. This same American parent who is uncertain about the sexual behavior that is right for his child is *also* not defining his child's adult career. Here, as in the sexual order, he encourages the child to find his own way by himself.

For an American adolescent to *choose* his specific adult identity (career, mate, sexual style) reverses the direction of the traditional socialization process. In traditional societies, adult identities are bestowed, not chosen. Adults decide what their children shall be. Moreover adult identities are definite and enduring. A youth is not allowed to create them by undertaking new responsibilities, innovating new situations, or generating his model from within himself. A traditional identity is bestowed upon youth from *outside;* but in America, an adult identity is chosen by a youth *for* and *by* himself. The modern youth selects his own career. He also selects his own marriage partner.

An example showing this consistency of methods used by a society to develop both career and sexual adulthoods is found in Laurence Wylie's essay on "Youth in France and the United States." Note the congruence between the French methods of initiating adolescents into both an adult vocation and adult sexual life:

CAREER IDENTITY

The average French child (and his parents even more than he) has a clear idea of the limits within which his ambition may be fulfilled. He knows to what social and professional class he belongs. There is no doubt about his family's traditional, political, religious, and even aesthetic ideals, and he has been placed by both family and teachers in a well-defined intellectual category. . . .[30]

SEXUAL IDENTITY

A traditional means has evolved in France for the indoctrination of young people in the expression of their sexual feelings. The adolescent boy receives his experience and training from an older woman and then in turn initiates the girl —ideally, of course, his virgin wife—in the art he has learned. French literature and movies offer examples of this. . . .[31]

Notice that, in French society, the confidence of the younger person about his sexual competence derives from the reassuring approval of an elder, a parent surrogate. On the basis of her experience, the elder woman assures a boy that he is now a man. This means that the confidence of the youth is a function of a dependency relationship. Hence, an adolescent does not develop self-confidence, or the ability to trust his own experience and choose for himself. His confidence is in the experience of his elders and he trusts their reassurance.

The French method of inculcating sexual maturity and confidence is similar to the French method of bestowing a career identity. Both methods presuppose the dependency of the younger upon the older generation and also reinforce this dependency. Were the younger generation to revolt against the older, it would be revolting against the very persons who are the foundation of its own confidence. In fact, the younger generation does not really have self-confidence. This is because its own confidence is really dependent upon the assurances of the adult generation. The younger generation has to believe the older generation is an authority because it has to trust the assurances of the older generation that it is really competent and mature. This psychosocial mechanism both explains the authoritarianism of traditional societies and accounts for their being "past-oriented" and slow to change.

America, however, as a society committed to change and innovation requires its youth to gain genuine self-confidence, a confidence in itself derived from youth's own experimentations and experience. Youth must become independent. It cannot repeat the past, trust the experience of its elders, or rely on their reassurance. Youth must chart its own way.

Such independence requires the development of self-confidence, *fidelity*, as the basis of adult identity.

An interesting presentation of the conflict between the traditional and modern methods of initiation to adulthood was presented in *The Graduate*. Benjamin, an adolescent boy, returns home from college. His parents give him a car and try to define his vocation for him. He should go into plastics. In parallel fashion, Benjamin is initiated into sexual adulthood by Mrs. Robinson, the wife of his father's business associate, a woman old enough to be his mother. (Even when in bed with her, he addresses her as "Mrs. Robinson.") Quite consistent with her initiative in seducing him, she also attempts to direct his relations with his female peers. The price Benjamin pays for having vocational and sexual adulthood bestowed upon him is to accept the direction for his life that those bestowing this adulthood prescribe for him. The parental forces in his life are treating him in the traditional way.

The theme of *The Graduate* is Benjamin's struggle to free himself from the parent figures who are seeking to bestow an identity upon him. In this struggle, he must learn how to be faithful to himself. Symbolically, he must abandon the automobile given to him and leave his parents' home. He must also create his own sexual maturity. He can do this only by "making it" with a girl as inexperienced as he, one of his peers. For when Benjamin "makes it" with her, he knows that he has really made it by himself!

Laurence Wylie, who described sexual and vocational initiation in France (above), contrasts the French with the American way: In France, he says, the adolescent boy receives his sexual experience and training from an older woman, but "to the American boy the very idea of sexual relations with a woman old enough to be his mother seems monstrous. He learns sexual techniques *just as he is taught to learn all things:* by venturing out, fumbling, experimenting, seeking advice from his peers or any other source he can find. Eventually, for better or for worse, he evolves his own system. . . . We have little information, but it appears that most American boys today receive their sexual initiation in the same situation with an older adolescent. . . . The whole clumsy operation may help account for the feeling of inadequacy shared by many American adults."[32]

The major difficulty with the American method, many feel, is that it may result in a permanent feeling of insecurity and lack of confidence if the sexual experience is not successful. To avoid such failures is, of course, the purpose of the graded development of intimacy by the method of petting, a graded development that is inculcated by a wide variety of institutional supports. For example, the occasional inspection of parked cars by police flashlights encourages the practice of petting, but inhibits both the removal of clothing and coitus. That such inhibitions do not totally prevent coitus is perfectly obvious. But this informally institutionalized procedure offers society's suggestion to the car parkers regarding the degree of intimacy that is acceptable, and it should be noted that, *within this limit,* the possibility of success is rather high.

The psychologist Bruno Bettelheim argues against the American method of sexual education by suggesting that the risk of failure and consequent injury to self-confidence is too great. Precisely because this need for self-esteem is so important, Bettelheim argues that the traditional method of sexual initiation is better.

[Bettelheim writes, "Laurence Wylie describes how, in a large segment of the French middle classes, the adolescent boy receives his training in love-making from an older woman . . . There is much more than simple experience involved in this way of teaching sex to an inexperienced young man. His very inexperience makes him attractive to the mature woman. In the typical American pattern, ignorance is supposed to be the best teacher of the ignorant in sexual matters. . . .

"American middle class youth learns about sex in the back seat of a car. . . . The first sexual experience often leaves ineffable impressions, marred by a total lack of experience on either side. Both partners feel anxious and insecure, neither one can offer encouragement to the other, nor can they take comfort from the accomplished sex act, since they cannot be sure that they did it well, all comparisons lacking."[33]]

"The young Frenchman," Bettelheim says, "not only knows that his inexperience makes him sexually attractive, he also receives the accolades of the person from whom it counts most: an experienced woman has found him not only sexually attractive, but from her rich experience (based on comparisons) she has also assured him that he is a manly lover indeed."[34]

Shades of Mrs. Robinson! The reader will be amused to note Bettelheim's blithe disregard of Wylie's remark that "the very idea of sexual relations with a woman old enough to be his mother seems monstrous" to the American boy. Precisely because the young American adolescent needs to be self-confident and free from such authority, his mother (the "experienced woman") is *not* the person whose accolades count most.

Bettelheim's comment does raise an important issue. Suppose it be granted that the experimental method of sexual initiation is more consistent with the other structures of American society. Does it follow from this fact alone that this method really works? For, as Bettelheim rightly points out, the psychological attachment of the child to his mother does seem to make this older person the one "whose accolade counts most." If this is the case, then how can a young man gain self-confidence through intimacy with an inexperienced girl his own age?

The answer to this question is, quite simply, that for the young man, the inexperienced girl his own age has to be the one "whose accolade counts most." The man must want her approval more than the approval of an older woman, and the adolescent woman must also want the approval of her peer-group boyfriend. Bettelheim does not see that this can be the case because *he still regards the adolescent as a child.* That is, Bettelheim still thinks of the adolescent as having his identity through his parents and within his family. He still thinks of the adolescent in a traditional way. But what has happened in America is that the adolescent no longer is a child and no longer has a primary family identity. The adolescent in America has "migrated" to a substitute primary group, a new social grouping of persons which is more important for him than his life in his family. This is the adolescent's peer group, a group of persons the same age, a group of his equals. Once this peer group is more important to an adolescent than his family, what counts the most to him is no longer the accolade of any more experienced elder. Now what counts the most to him is the approval of his equally inexperienced peers —with whom, through conversation and trial and error, he gradually learns those competences necessary to his being a free and autonomous adult.

[The overcoming of dependency upon authority and the gaining of self-confidence is made possible by learning how to manage peer-group relations—namely, learning how to have friends and relate to equals. It is the characteristic mark of an authoritarian person that he is able to relate well only to persons "higher" or "lower" than he. Whenever he encounters an equal, he is psychologically constrained to compete with him and try to outdo him—or to be outdone. This competition makes it impossible for the authoritarian-oriented person to regard any equal as a friend—or to accept any equal as fully and finally equal.

This is why, for example, authoritarian persons have so much difficulty in, and fear of, sensitivity groups. In sensitivity groups there is no hierarchical structure and every person is an equal. The authoritarian person finds such a social situation destroys his basic identity orientation. But in such groups, he can also begin to understand the psychological mechanism that locks him into his behavior and, finally, makes him so lonesome and friendless. For example, here is a typical comment from one person who had suddenly seen the connection of these things. "I have never had any trouble with authority. I always did very well in school and never got into trouble. In fact, whenever it came to any competition I was always near the top. But somehow I never seemed to have any friends— and I'm so lonely." Or, a more angry and liberated example, "I used to get along with the System fine. I kissed everybody's ass—my teacher's, my captain's, my boss'. But I didn't have any friends then. Then one day I said 'To Hell with all this Bull Shit.' And now I've got hundreds of friends. I can't figure out why.' "

What happened, in the second case, was not that the man involved began misbehaving. Rather, he simply disengaged himself psychologically from authoritarian relationships and discovered that he was now psychologically capable of managing equalitarian friendships.]

In Europe and in other traditional societies, the parent-child bond remains strong all through adolescence. Adolescent peers do not constitute themselves an independent "counter-family"—a group that serves to diminish the child's attachment to his parents. In America, however, adolescents constitute themselves into independent "counter-families." These peer groups are the setting for psychological, social, and sexual experimentation and growth. Such peer groups resemble, in fact, the ancient male groups—with one significant difference. Membership in them is heterosexual. Hence, they are suitable settings for sexual learning.

It must be admitted that the sexual learning by experimentation that takes place in these groups is fraught with difficulty, and that the American adolescent may be more anxious and insecure than adolescents in traditional societies. But this arises from the fact that in his sexual education, as in all his adolescent experience, he is being encouraged to be generally independent and to accumulate, be guided by, and trust in his own experience. The kind of personal and sexual confidence that he needs to gain is not to know that he can satisfy Mommy and Daddy, but to know that he can stand independently, control his world, evolve his own methods, and, finally, choose his own adulthood. Needless to say, he must endure more anxiety and uncertainty throughout this learning process than his French cousin. But the question must be raised whether the elimination of such uncertainty by returning him to the condition of dependency is worth the price. Obviously it is not. For America, as a changing innovative society, requires the development of self-confidence, or fidelity, as the basis of personal identity and autonomous adulthood.

Earlier in this volume, it was pointed out that one of the effects of romantic love is to make the parent-child relation less important than the husband-wife relation. In traditional societies, the parent-child relation is primary—so that the husband and the wife finally come to be related to each other through their children. In American society, on the other hand, the husband-wife relation is more important than the parent-child role (at least wherever the principle of romantic marriage has not been compromised). In American society, the husband and father roles are kept distinct—as are the roles of wife and mother. Even where women lapse into total domesticity, there is a high premium on their remaining the peers of, and companions of, their husbands. The husband

and wife hope, as an ideal, to have a direct personal relation that is not dependent on their relation to their children.

The emergence of adolescent peer groups—as alternative primary social units where youths can establish identity and learn morality by themselves—is the counterfacing balance to this romantic husband-wife relation. Just as an American husband and wife have their private relation and their friends apart from their relation to their children, so their children have their friends and intense personal relations quite apart from their relation to their parents. Just as the parents do not need the children in order to be related to each other, so adolescents do not depend upon their parents to grow to adulthood. The adolescent peer group makes the adolescent's relation to his parents as secondary as the romantic marriage makes the parents' relation to their children. (The general tendency, moreover, is to extend the peer group principle to younger and younger ages. At present, "preadolescent peer groups" are beginning to appear. An example of this tendency can be seen in the recent decisions of the Boy Scouts and Girl Scouts to lower all the entrance ages.)

The greater importance of the husband-wife relation in American society has a transforming effect on the character of the marriage relation, too. In a traditional society, where parents are related to each other through the children, the husband-wife relation is easily described as the fulfillment of definite social roles. If to be a husband is to be a father (and to be a father is to support a family), then the "proof" that a man loves his wife is that he brings home the bacon. And if to be a wife is to be a mother (and the role of a mother is to bear and care for children), then the "proof" that a woman loves her husband is that she bears his children. In both these cases, the love between a husband and a wife is expressed as the fulfillment of precise social roles.

When, however, the husband-wife relation is direct and not identified with the father-mother relation, the love of husband and wife can no longer be expressed by fulfilling a social role. It now must be intimate and personal. But for intimate personal love to exist between a man and a woman, each must have learned a capacity for personal fidelity and heterosexual equality. Each must have learned to integrate sexual desires with personal love. Each must truly enjoy the other and find in their communion and sharing the fulfillment of love. It is not simply "natural" to do these things. The capacity to do them must be developed and a certain moral taste must be learned. As we have seen, these new capacities and tastes are learned in the heterosexual peer group where adolescents learn to relate to one another as friends and discover how to manage nonaggressive sex.

We see, therefore, a certain pattern of mutually supportive institutions. The capacity for heterosexual intimacy and the taste for communitive sexual relation is learned within the peer group. Persons who have learned these capacities can then manage romantic-personal marriage and need not use their children to relate to each other as husband and wife. Because they do not use their children to relate to each other, they can then allow their children the degree of freedom necessary for the children to join their own peer groups. The children then begin to gain independent identities and learn the psychosocial skills presupposed by romantic marriage. In this way, the pattern turns full circle.

Part Four

THE QUESTION

CHAPTER X

Sex Without Sex?

WE HAVE now traced the evolution of human sexuality through several stages and can, at this point, notice certain long-range tendencies. There is, first, a tendency toward the *moralization of sex*. By this is meant the displacement of instinctual agression as the fundamental sexual drive by the feeling of voluntary shared love. There is, second, a tendency toward the *individuation of men and women*. By this is meant the gradual process of growth in self-understanding whereby men and women come to recognize one another not simply as equals, but as beings containing within themselves the possibility for full identification with the feelings of the other sex. There is, third, a tendency toward the *eroticization of society*. By this is meant the freeing of sexual feeling from its locus in the genitals of the body and the diffusion of that feeling throughout all human interaction so that even business and political activities will not be impersonal, but friendly and "warm."

Having considered these three general tendencies that have appeared in our study of the evolution of human sexuality, can we go on to predict the future? It seems clear that, although we are coming to the end of this book on sexual evolution, sexual evolution itself will go further. The American romantic marriage and the parent/child (two-generation) family cannot be regarded as the fulfillment of this evolutionary process —if only because these institutions are tightly bound up with an aggressive-possessive economic system that must also be superseded if man is to survive. It is important to realize that the attitudes, virtues, and goals presupposed by aggressive-possessive capitalism do tend to form a person who possesses only a limited capacity for personal intimacy and heterosexual sharing. (The Women Liberationists are correct in their estimate that American capitalism is patriarchal, for hierarchical patriarchy reinforces the competitive orientation that thinks in terms of moving "higher" and getting "ahead.") What this means, therefore, is that there is a disequilibrium among American *institutional ideals*. A highly competitive economy reinforces residual patriarchal, nonequalitarian tendencies in the sexual sphere—where such patriarchal tendencies run contrary to the professed personal-romantic ideal. This disequilibrium will gradually be corrected by the emergence of new communal forms of economic organization.

It is beyond the scope of this book to engage in futurology. The process of evolution is always introducing novel elements into human affairs that, before they appeared, could hardly have been anticipated. I believe that present-day sexual experimentation is a more or less conscious search for some new break-through. But it is not my present interest to distinguish genuinely promising from totally ridiculous experiments. Rather than offer a look into the future, therefore, let me close with a look into the past. For it is in the past, especially in the American utopian tradition that flourished in the nineteenth century, that I believe we may discover hints about the way that we should seek to go.

The American utopian communities of the eighteenth and nineteenth centuries were not simply religious in inspiration, but were really further developments of the medieval monastic tradition. In American utopianism as in medieval monasticism, men sought to create a new form of human community on the basis of a new spirituality (new human consciousness) that also produced a new mode of sexuality. In medieval monasticism, men sought to create new more inclusive communities by rejecting the partialities of the biological family—renouncing sexual intercourse and raising celibacy to an ideal. In certain of the more important American utopias, there was the searching for a more universal form of human community through the *communalization,* rather than the renunciation, of sex. Let us consider some examples.

The most important of the American monastic communities is the Shakers. This community was founded in the eighteenth century and survived until the middle of the twentieth. The Shakers were communistic and agricultural, their settlements being scattered throughout the eastern part of the United States. Shaker communalism was unlike medieval monasticism on four essential points. (1) Work was more highly valued, being regarded as a form of highest human fulfillment and an intrinsic act of glorifying God. The Shakers were important innovators and inventors in American history, even though their work was not motivated by competition and desire for private profit. (2) The Shaker communities were communistic heterosexual groups where all the men and women were related to one another equally. Men and women lived together and worked together and danced together—though coital intercourse itself was explicitly renounced. The atmosphere of such communities and the comportment of the different persons toward one another was, many commentators noticed, affectionate and warm. (The renunciation of sexual intercourse does not, of itself, mean the renunciation of sexual feeling.) (3) Shakers believed in a God who has both Motherly and Fatherly characteristics, and they also believed in two Messiahs: the man Jesus Christ and the woman Mother Ann Lee (their founder). We have already considered the importance of such twofold symbolism for the affirmation that men *qua* males and women *qua* females are not only equal to, but also fully "images" of, one another. (4) The Shakers practiced, as their characteristic ritual, a heterosexual "shaking dance" that provided regular "orgasmic release." Modern psychology now judges the kind of tension release attained by ecstatic shaking to be the equivalent, physiologically speaking, of coital orgasm.

From this point of view, Shaker ecstatic dancing was a kind of communal sexual interaction and orgasm that could, in principle, satisfy the normal physiological need for tension release. Moreover, it also met the psychological need of persons for heightened heterosociality.

What is striking about the Shaker communities is that they enjoyed and appreciated the natural world and the human body, yet they did not do so by glorifying genital sex and idolatrizing the biological family. Rather, they created a new, more inclusive mode of heterosociality and they evolved a living institution that overcame the partialities of the traditional family group. The partialities of the traditional biological family are (a) that it limits the number of intimate male-female relationships to the spouses, (b) that it is based upon the accumulation of private property and creates a distinction between the rich and the poor, and (c) that it requires women to be relegated to the status of household help. The Shakers overcame these limitations by creating a communalistic economy and family which was bound together by the ritual-sexual act of ecstatic "shaking."

It is worth questioning our ordinary presuppositions, at this point, and asking ourselves whether such ecstatic dancing is really only an intrinsically deficient substitute for genital intercourse, or whether it is an intrinsically superior mode of sexual interaction of which ordinary intercourse is but an inferior anticipation. Is it the case that coital intercourse is the basic, complete, and total sexual act for which ecstatic dancing can be only the merest "sublimation"? Or might it be the case that ecstatic dancing comes closer to the full and most intense form of sexual communication, in relation to which genital intercourse can be only regarded as an impoverished "segmentation"? Norman Brown, for example, rejects the concentration of sex in a genital act and calls for the total sexualization of the body. Such a totally sexualized body might be a body engaged in ecstatic heterosocial dancing. Such dancing is total intercourse, rather than merely genital intercourse. The Shakers, I believe, were practical innovators in human sexuality—and discovered something akin to what Brown has been calling for: the reeroticization of the body and the total life of man. That such a development could go hand in hand with Shaker celibacy (that is, renunciation of coital intercourse) is quite understandable. For the renunciation of genital intercourse is also the renunciation of the genital organization of the body and opens the way for a new polymorphous total sexuality to emerge.

Everything in this book drives us to the conclusion that genital sexual activity is but a part of some larger, yet more intimate, human communication. The Shakers, by their celibacy, found their way into a higher, more complex, more satisfying form of sex. Such a conclusion may startle those for whom the basic and complete form of human sexuality is coital intercourse and genital orgasm. But it forces us to ask ourselves once again the question: Is it the Shakers or is it we who are _really_ sexually repressed?

A second American utopian group, no less interesting than the Shakers, was the Oneida Community established in New York and Connecticut in the nineteenth century by John Humphrey Noyes. Noyes was trained as a Congregationalist minister and under the influence of the revival spirit set out to establish a new kind of utopian group. Oneida, unlike the Shaker communities, was not agricultural, but self-consciously industrial in its economic base. It invested much of the community funds in the education of its members in technical skills. Like the Shakers, the Oneida Community was communistic, rejecting monogamy and private property. But unlike the Shakers, the Oneida Community did not reject sexual intercourse. Rather, Noyes created a new form of sexual relationship which he called "complex marriage." Within complex marriage, sexual intercourse was permitted among all the members of the community though the purpose of such liaisons was purely "amative" rather than "procreative." Noyes believed, with some justification, that such amative sexual unions reinforced the personal bonds among the members of the community.

For such amative unions to take place, and to keep them sharply distinguished from the procreative use of sex, a distinctive method of "contraception" was employed—which Noyes called "Male Continence." Strictly speaking, Male Continence was not a method of contraception. Rather, it was a method of avoiding ejaculation and _male_ orgasm, a practice that totally transforms the meaning and purpose of the sexual act. It is important to emphasize this point. Male Continence had, as its effect, the shifting of the purpose of the sexual act from excitation and tension release—a purely private pleasure—to the continued communion, heightened mutual awareness, and shared enjoyment of the partners. We have already seen that such Male Continence was practiced by courtly lovers as a means of heightening the intimacy and communion between them without allowing the personal-sexual union to fall under instinctual control. We have also seen that this method of sexual union (called *maithuna*) was practiced in ancient India as a way of religiosexual contemplation, a way of winning heightened awareness of another and enjoying "God" in and through him or her.

Male Continence, *maithuna*, and the techniques of courtly love are not, therefore, simple methods of contraception. They are, rather, ways of fundamentally transforming the purpose and experience of sex itself. Aldous Huxley, in his utopian novel *Island*, specifically describes this new experience of sex. "What is maithuna?" someone asks. And the following conversation ensues:

"Basically, maithuna is the same as what the Oneida people called Male Continence. And that was the same as what Roman Catholics mean by *coitus reservatus*. . . ."

"In a word," Will concluded, "it's just birth control without contraceptives."

"But that is only the beginning of the story," said Ranga. "Maithuna is also something else. Something even more important. . . . What we're born with, what we experience all through infancy and childhood is a sexuality that isn't concentrated on the genitals; it's a sexuality diffused through the whole organism. That's the paradise we inherit. But the paradise gets lost as the child grows up. Maithuna is the organized attempt to regain that paradise."[35]

The purpose of *maithuna*—and the experience following from Male Continence—is, therefore, totally different from that sexual intercourse that aims at orgasm. Ordinary orgasmic intercourse presupposes and reinforces the genital organization of the body. It is a form of segmental sex. But there is a form of sexual union that seeks to overcome this genital sex and reeroticize the entire body. This is the "amative inter-course" of the Oneida Community. And in its seeking to overcome the genital segmentation of sex and attain to the sexualization of the entire body, this method of sexual interaction resembles the ecstatic dancing that was practiced among the Shakers.

There is, however, a difference between the ecstatic dancing of the Shakers and the Male Continence (or *maithuna*) of the Oneida Community. I have already noted that the ecstatic dancing of the Shakers was a kind of "orgasmic release." In Male Continence, however, the male orgasm is withheld. The goal of the sexual union is not orgasm, tension release, something *else*. The goal of sexual union is that very union, communion, and mutual contemplation. This leads us to see that the essence of this new form of sexual union is the heightened control over the instinctual sexual processes by the human intelligence and will. This heightened control does not involve the repression of sexual feeling, but its perfect integration with the voluntary capacities of man. It involves what we have called "the moralization, or voluntarization, of sex."

Huxley, in *Island,* quotes Spinoza's dictum in describing *maithuna.* "Make," Spinoza said, "the body capable of doing many things. This will help you to perfect the mind and so to come to the intellectual love of God." The practice of *maithuna* is seen as a way of raising the mind toward God. John Humphrey Noyes, in a somewhat different way, stresses the voluntarization of sex that occurs through the practice of Male Continence. Noyes argues that sexual intercourse does not require the final stage of orgasm, and that the process of sexual union is so at man's command that he can choose or withhold orgasm at any point. Writes Noyes:

Now we insist that this whole process, up to the very moment of emission, is *voluntary,* entirely under the control of the moral faculty, and *can be stopped at any point.* In other words, the *presence* and the *motions* can be continued or stopped at will, and it is only the final *crisis* of emission that is automatic or uncontrollable. . . . If you say that this is impossible, I answer that I *know* it is possible—nay, that it is easy.[36]

In these texts, we see that there is an intrinsic relationship between the further development of certain of those tendencies discerned in our consideration of the history of sexuality. There is a relation between the resexualization of the body and the voluntarization of sex.

A third utopian community, no less important than either the Shakers or the Oneida group, was the Mormons. During the period of their settlement in Nauvoo, Illinois, Joseph Smith, their leader, introduced the idea that there is a second form of marriage that is totally different from traditional temporal marriage. In 1843, Smith publicly taught, or alluded to the secret rite, that there is such a thing as a "celestial marriage." In a sermon on this topic, Smith taught that

Except a man and his wife enter into an everlasting covenant and be married for eternity, while in this probation [life], by the power and authority of the Holy Priesthood, they will cease to increase when they die; that is, they will have no children after the resurrection. But those who are [so] married and continue without committing the sin against the Holy Ghost, will continue to increase and have children in the celestial glory.[37]

Celestial marriage is a personal-sexual union that has eternal value and will exist forever. The very notion of such a celestial marriage presupposes that men and women have become aware of themselves as spiritual beings, as beings whose meaning and purpose are not determined by the temporal, biological order about them. The notion of celestial marriage makes clear that sex and procreation are not essentially biological, but are spiritual acts.

The Mormon doctrine of celestial marriage, like the medieval doctrine of the immaculate conception of Mary, is a symbol of the emergence of a wholly new consciousness in man. In an earlier chapter, we saw that the doctrine of the immaculate conception was a doctrinal way of symbolizing that perfect moral sinlessness, the power fully to transcend one's biological existence, is present no less in women than it is in men. The doctrine of the immaculate conception was a symbolic way of equalizing the relationship between men and women, a symbolization that came to practical expression in the institution of courtly love. In the same way, the Mormon doctrine of celestial marriage is a symbolic way of expressing a new self-understanding and communicating a new understanding of the possibilities open to human sexuality. This doctrine is a symbolic way of affirming that the sexual is but the expression of the spiritual, that the temporal is but a medium of the eternal, and that man, by his freedom, can engage in divine creation.

Still more important, however, is that the doctrine of celestial marriage is a symbolic way of drawing those consequences involved in man's increasing awareness of himself as a unique person ("the individuation of man"). As we have seen, this awareness that each individual man is an absolutely unique person—unlike any other and absolutely irreplaceable—did not emerge until the modern period of history. To be aware of each person as unique is for man to be fully self-conscious and self-creative. Before the modern period of history, human beings did not think of each individual person as unique. Rather, humans felt themselves to be all representatives of a single class. From this point of view, every woman was essentially like every other woman—and every man was essentially like every other man. One good wife merely did what any other good wife would do. Hence, so long as this feeling reigned, it was to be expected that marriage should be assumed to be merely a temporal contract. Once a wife dies, another may be taken. Once a husband dies, another may be had. In Catholic Christianity, for example, divorce is forbidden but remarriage following the death of either spouse is allowed. This means that the Catholic Church (like most Protestant churches) regards marriage as a purely temporal institution. The partners are bound together only for time. Their *marital* relation is not a celestial, or everlasting, one.

Joseph Smith, on the other hand, denied that the highest form of marriage is such a temporal—and limited—union. He sensed that a relationship between two unique persons cannot be dissolved, but must itself be a spiritual reality. He sensed that death cannot dissolve such a union. And because the essence of marriage, according to Smith, is spiritual, he also concluded that a plural number of such spiritual relations might be not only legitimate, but even desirable. This idea of a plural number of spiritual relations becomes something very akin to the ancient aspiration toward a single family of man.

It is a matter of dispute whether Smith himself ever understood his notion of celestial marriage to mean that a plural number of sexual liaisons are also permitted within this temporal life. That is, it is not clear whether Smith would have ever consented to the explicit developments in Mormonism that took place after his death—namely, the emergence of polygamy. For Smith was killed shortly after he developed his teaching on celestial marriage, and the interpretation of his teaching has, ever since, remained a point of dispute between the two continuing Mormon groups.

It is clear, however, that after Smith's death and the forced emigration of the Mormons to Utah under the leadership of Brigham Young, the teaching on celestial marriage was understood to imply the legitimacy of polygamy. Throughout the nineteenth century, polygamy was widely practiced by the Utah Mormons. Such a development of doctrine and practice is a well-known phenomenon in all religious traditions. For the Utah Mormons, this development reflected their need to adapt to persecution and immigration as facts of life. Polygamy was the basis of the new tribal life the Mormons were forced to undertake in the wilderness.

Whether Smith's teaching would have developed in this way if the Nauvoo group had not been persecuted is an interesting, but unresolvable, question. Suffice it to note that the doctrine of celestial marriage, with the magnificent vision of the meaning of marriage and human sexuality it implies, is in no way dependent upon, or logically tied to, polygamy. Rather, it is a way of speaking of the eternality and unrepeatability of every marital and sexual union—a way of expressing man's new consciousness of himself as a unique spiritual being. In these respects, Smith's teaching resembles the new visions that were also emerging in other American utopias, especially in the Shaker and Oneida communities.

I believe these American utopian experiments are suggestive about the further evolution of sexuality. They all began with the Puritan-spiritualist vision, but further developed and communalized it. In these utopias we see possible developments of the characteristic tendencies discovered in our earlier pages: the further moralization of sex, the further individuation of man, and the further eroticization of society. If, in concluding, we were to ask the kinds of prerequisites that must be present in order for further evolution to take place, I believe—from this book— we could single out the following points:

First, there can be no further evolution of sexuality that is not also the expression of a new mode of human consciousness. This is because, as we have seen, every vision about transformed society and human behavior presupposes some determinate self-awareness of man. This self-awareness contains within itself all the possibilities that man can imagine as open to himself. Without an evolution of human consciousness, there cannot be, therefore, any evolution of sexuality. Every evolution in the sexual order presupposes, and only expresses, an evolution that has first of all taken place in the spiritual order.

In this book, we have seen the forms of sexuality that have been expressive of mimetic, ego, rational, and self-consciousness respectively. The new form of consciousness that must emerge before men can manage the more complex communalization of sex hinted at by the American utopias must be a kind of "polyconsciousness." It must be a consciousness whereby men can somehow find that sharing does not threaten themselves and their individualities, a consciousness that is able to bear a greater multiplicity in unity. I do not know precisely what such a consciousness would be. But it is clear that some such emergence must first precede the institutionalization of any such communal sexuality as has been hinted at above.

Second, there can be no evolution of human sexuality without some "lead time" experimentation by a disciplined spiritual-sexual elite. Some small group must not only *envision* a new possibility, but must also organize to try and reach it. Without the discipline to organize itself into an organic community within which the new sexual attitudes can be sustained and the new sexual behavior be practiced, such a group cannot innovate, but can only dream. It may be possible for one person to paint a picture or cultivate a garden by himself. But no single person or couple can innovate a new style of sexual behavior, for sexuality is a complicated social phenomenon and always presupposes at least a minimally representative community as its basic unit. Hence, when we consider the whole history of sexuality, we see that the great evolutionary "leaps" were innovated and established by small but disciplined religious communities which sensed the new spiritual possibility open to man and sought to give this vision practical expression in a reformed society. The three great pioneering elites were, of course, the ancient Hebrews, the Catholic monastics, and the American Puritans and spiritualists. In the same way, we have seen the continued struggle of religious elites attempting to form disciplined communities that could sustain new sexual ideals in the American utopian tradition. The Shakers, the Oneida Community, and the Mormons all have attempted to reach beyond what they had received and raise man toward some new possibility. What can now be done will necessarily have to build on this tradition.

Finally, the next evolution of human sexuality will not destroy the moral and social achievements of the past, but will build upon them. This next stage will not be so much a "something else" as it will be a "something more." The process of evolution is not a process of revolution. Were one to destroy the past with every innovation, there could be no increase and no development. Evolution takes place only as something more is added to what has been. Development comes only as we build upon the past rather than destroying it. Human history is an augmentative process. Things "complexify" as the new is added to the old, thereby creating some new mixture. Hence, I do not anticipate a radical reversal of the values and achievements of the past. I do not anticipate a repudiation of the personal-intimate character of sexual love, a rejection of the private-exclusive relation, or a return to authoritarian family systems. Rather, I anticipate the universalization and ratification of the values and trends that we have seen emerging—though this must occur through some new organizing vision.

NOTES

1. Paul Brohmer, "The New Biology: Training in Racial Citizenship," *Nazi Culture*, ed. G. Mosse (New York, 1966), 87 f.
2. Lewis Mumford, *The City in History* (New York, 1961), 42.
3. J. Edgar Bruns, "Some Early Historical Development of New Testament Morality," *The New Morality*, ed. W. Dunphy (New York, 1967), 76.
4. M. Esther Harding, *The "I" and the "Not-I"* (New York, 1965), 140 f.
5. *Ibid.*, 38 f., 49 f.
6. Theodore Lidz, *The Person* (New York, 1968), 424.
7. *Ibid.*
8. Derrick Sherwin Bailey, *Sexual Relation in Christian Thought* (New York, 1959), 33 f.
9. Michael Balint, *Die Urformen der Liebe und die Technik der Psychoanalyse* (Frankfurt am Main, 1970), 125.
10. A Kinsey *et al.*, *Sexual Behavior in the Human Female* (New York, 1953), 254 f.
11. Morton Hunt, *The Natural History of Love* (New York, 1959), 141 f.
12. Ralph Waldo Emerson, "Love," *Essays*, ed. S. Paul (London, 1967), 103 f.
13. *The Church Today (Gaudium et Spes)*, ch. 50. *The Documents of Vatican II*, ed. W. Abbott (New York, 1966), 253 f.
14. Erik Erikson, *Insight and Responsibility* (New York, 1964), 84.
15. Dietrich Haensch, *Repressiven Familienpolitik* (Hamburg, 1969), 84. The translation is extremely paraphrastic.
16. Max Horkheimer, "Autorität und Familie," *Traditionelle und kritische Theorie* (Frankfurt am Main, 1970), 216.
17. James Sellers, *Public Ethics* (New York, 1970), 82 f.
18. Hunt, *Op. cit.*, 142.
19. Freud's view that genital and pregenital love are aspects of the same physio-

logical system is now known to be false. See Michael Balint, *Op. cit.*, ch. 1–4.

20. Harvey Cox, "A Brothel in Noble Dimensions," *Sex, Family, and Society in Theological Focus*, ed. J. C. Winn (New York, 1965), 54.

21. Ira Reiss, *Premarital Sexual Standards in America* (New York, 1960), 233.

22. Rustum and Della Roy, *Honest Sex* (New York, 1969), 101 f.

23. Reiss, *Op. cit.*, 229.

24. *Ibid.*, 133 f.

25. *Ibid.*

26. *Ibid.*

27. Alan Watts, *Nature, Man, and Woman* (New York, 1958), 160–169.

28. Erikson, *Op. cit.*, 137.

29. *Ibid.*, 127 f.

30. Laurence Wylie, "Youth in France and the United States," *The Challenge of Youth*, ed. E. Erikson (New York, 1965), 298.

31. *Ibid.*, 310 f.

32. *Ibid.*, 296 f.

33. Bruno Bettelheim, "The Problem of Generations," *The Challenge of Youth* (New York, 1965), 98 f.

34. *Ibid.*, 296 f.

35. Aldous Huxley, *Island* (New York, 1962), 86–89.

36. Cited from Marin Lockwood Carden, *Oneida* (Baltimore, 1969), 49 f.

37. Cited from Robert Flanders, *Nauvoo: Kingdom on the Mississippi* (Urbana, 1965), 272.

INDEX